The 21st Century Christian

SEEKING UNCHANGEABLE TRUTHS IN AN EVER-CHANGING WORLD

JT ALEXANDER

Copyright © 2014 by JT Alexander

All rights reserved. No part of this publication may be reproduced, distributed or transmitted in any form or by any means, including photocopying, recording, or other electronic or mechanical methods, without the prior written permission of the publisher, except in the case of brief quotations embodied in critical reviews and certain other noncommercial uses permitted by copyright law.

J.T. Alexander
P.O. Box 24
Etiwanda, CA 91739-0024
email: **21cc@jtalex.com**
www.jtalex.com
Cover Design (graphics) by J.T. Alexander ©2014

Ordering Information:
For details on larger orders, please contact
J.T. Alexander at the address or email shown above.

21st Century Christian/ J.T. Alexander —1st ed.
ISBN: 1494755084
ISBN-13: 9781494755089
Library of Congress Control Number: 2013923449
CreateSpace Independent Publishing Platform
North Charleston, South Carolina
Title ID: 4582176

Acknowledgements

At the outset, I'd like to express my love and gratitude for my wife, Heather, who has always been an encouragement through every project I've undertaken. Also, my love and appreciation for our sons, Nathan and Gabriel, their families, and our extended family members. And an endless thanksgiving for the years that we all shared with Joselyn, before she was taken from us.

I am eternally grateful for my parents, John and Millie Alexander, whose prayers and steadfast faith blessed my life in countless and unforeseen ways.

Additionally, many thanks to my editor and friend, Bill Ireland. His knowledge and guidance helped me put forth my best effort to overcome a good deal of apprehension about writing this, my first book.

Table of Contents

Acknowledgements iii

Introduction vii

Thought and Confusion 1

The Problem With Truth 7

The God Who Is 21

The Perpetual Force 37

The Prelude to Prayer 49

The Good Ol' Days 63

The Power Behind Humility 71

Fear 85

Politics and Religion 101

The End Game 115

Concluding Thoughts 143

Introduction

You now find yourself in the twenty-first century; in a world where media often tells you what to think and how to think about it. Never before has there been such a magnitude of conflicting voices that compete for your worldview. Everyone from educators to news anchors, pastors to politicians, bloggers to celebrities—anyone with access to a public forum—diligently work to shape the opinions of others. Now, a new time is emerging when *normal* is quickly being transformed into something yet unknown.

But what do *you* think of all the voices of conflicting opinions? Have you been able to come to a place of certainty in your own worldview?

Socrates' proclamation, "The unexamined life is not worth living," presents an essential truth for our time. For this reason, I wrote *The 21st Century Christian*. The journey begins with my own state of confusion about life's universal questions and traverses over the bumpy terrain of ambiguity to a place of certainty and confidence.

This book is written for anyone—Christian or nonbeliever—who possesses that essential ingredient for seeking truth in life: intellectual honesty. And why would we seek truth? In the words of George Mallory who climbed Mt. Everest, "Because it's there."

Truth exists, only falsehood has to be invented.

— Georges Braque, *Pensées sur l'art*

CHAPTER ONE

Thought and Confusion

From my vantage point, it looked like a beautiful day in the skies over South Vietnam, but I instinctively knew that the view was about to change. It was 1970 and the war was entering its final chapter. In three more years, the decade-long conflict would wind down as American troops were pulled out of Vietnam. But on this day, isolated battles continued around the country and nothing was certain.

The four-man medevac helicopter crew that I accompanied was en route to a landing zone just outside of Da Lot to provide aid and assistance. I had no official capacity on this mission and was simply documenting everything with my Petri 35mm fixed lens camera. After being airborne for about twenty minutes, we closed in on our destination. I looked out the UH-1 Huey's side compartment window and saw a small vertically-shaped cloud of purple smoke rising from an open field. It marked the area where an Army infantry patrol wanted us to land. The chopper descended, abruptly turned and maneuvered into position; its long main rotors pounding the air. The crew chief pulled the side door back and I was suddenly exposed to outdoor space. About ten feet from touching down, there was a large explosion, throwing dirt and rocks inside the chopper's bay where I sat with the medic and crew chief.

The Huey reflexed to the left and before I knew it, we were back in the air, far above the instant mayhem. I had never before realized how fast a UH-1 could climb and my mind was racing to catch up with the action. The medic leaned towards me, "We're not under attack," he assured. "We set off a booby trap." The strong downwash from our main rotors had activated one of several hidden explosives, planted beforehand by the Viet Cong. Fortunately, no one was injured from the blast and our trustworthy Huey remained unscarred.

One of the soldiers on the ground activated a second purple smoke canister on a nearby paved road, marking a safer place for us to land. We touched down with the cargo door open and facing the field, ready to receive our wounded passenger. Momentarily, a couple of infantrymen had their buddy on a stretcher and heading for the chopper—their lieutenant following close behind. As they approached, I could plainly see that the young man on the stretcher was in serious condition; his face torn and bloody. I later discovered that he had set off an explosive device by attempting to retrieve a booby-trapped AK-47 enemy assault rifle lying in the field.

Once the injured man was loaded onboard, the side door was latched closed and we were airborne. The medic did his best to administer aid to the bleeding soldier, but it was to no avail. About five minutes into the return flight, the medic placed a blanket over the young victim's head and body. It was at that moment I discovered something very troubling about myself.

The flight back to Phan Rang was quiet and uneventful. Under more favorable circumstances, the crew would be cracking jokes, or the pilots might make a low pass over tiny Vietnamese fishing boats for the fun of it. But this was a solemn trip and everyone seemed lost in their thoughts. I gazed over the landscape below and wondered what ever happened to my emotions. Why was I so disconnected from the tragedy that had taken the life of this young soldier, whose dead body was lying at my feet? Did he die for a good cause? Did a god exist to receive his eternal soul? Did he even *have* a soul? If not, what was the significance of anything I had just witnessed? Everything seemed so pointless.

I THINK, THEREFORE I AM—CONFUSED

The penned words of French philosopher, René Descartes, "Cogito ergo sum", or "I think, therefore I am," have survived for centuries because they reveal an indisputable truth. Descartes was simply offering the reality of thought as the evidence of being. But much of life's endless array of mysteries seemed perplexing to me. I had come to believe that confusion is our first inheritance, and we work within its maze seeking clues to truth and solutions to problems.

It never would have dawned on me in earlier life, but I must have been born with a philosopher's gene. From as far back as I can remember, I wanted to have a keener understanding of why things happened in the way that they did. Unfortunately, that curiosity didn't translate into a disciplined study habit until much later in life.

My first real philosophical struggle began at the point of a common childhood fascination. It all started with my first obsession to uncover the mystery behind that great holiday question: Is there really a Santa Claus? No one ever loved Christmas more than I did. I loved everything about this marvelous time of year: the tree and lights, the snow, the music, the baby Jesus, and of course, the presents under the tree. But as my childhood incrementally passed with each year, it was the origin of those presents under the tree that began to pique my interest.

Early on, my parents led me to believe that Santa Claus was the source of my Christmas morning euphoria, and I had seen plenty of story books with the fat man's jolly smile, tireless reindeer, and intercontinental sleigh. But I was getting to the age where the Santa story was causing me a bit of concern.

Something about that Christmas tale didn't seem fully plausible, although I could never quite put my finger on the problem. In time, I felt compelled to get to the bottom of this mystery; but first, I would have to devise a way to prove, once and for all, whether Santa Claus was fact or fiction—and there would be no peace on earth until I found the answer.

I was born in the South, but grew up in the North. My father's work brought our family from the Atlanta area to Detroit, Michigan when I was three. It was the early 1950s and Motown was the pride and joy of America's industrial age. Our home was a small, two-story structure with a simple design, but I never saw it as a modest abode. We had the only double lot in our working class neighborhood and the big backyard hosted many family events and neighborhood games of various types over the years.

As a boy, I always loved the four distinct seasons of Michigan. Neighbors would rake and burn their leaves at the curb during the weeks of autumn. The smoky odor filled the air and signaled an approaching holiday season. The days were getting shorter and colder. Before long, the snow would begin to fall.

Finally, it was the year of my grand scheme to prove, once and for all, whether Old St. Nick was the real deal. The stage was set. Christmas Eve had arrived and the decorated tree was standing in our living room in all its glory. I had asked my mother if it would be okay to set out a slice of her chocolate cake with a glass of milk and place it under the tree with a note to let Santa know that the dessert was intended for him. The plot was simple, but foolproof. If Santa partook of the treat, the evidence of his existence would be obvious and undeniable. But if the cake and milk were untouched, I would have to explore other possible avenues to discover how those toys got under my Christmas tree in the middle of the night.

On the glorious morning of discovery, I descended from my upstairs bedroom to find an empty glass and a half-eaten chocolate cake. The question had briefly crossed my mind, *why didn't Santa eat the whole thing?* But the facts were in: There really was a Santa Claus! Now, Christmas was not only splendid, it was resolved.

At some point between my creative detective work and the following Christmas, reality set in. It became very apparent to me that it was, in fact, my dad who had eaten the cake and drank the milk. And it had been my dad who had placed those gifts under the tree—year after year. Looking back, I should have been very grateful to both my parents for their love, sacrifice, and benevolence; but gratitude was something that eluded my self-centered mind at that age.

My love for Christmas continued, but the curiosity of this holiday shifted to that other story: the one about Jesus and how he came into the world to save humanity from its sinful state. That was the genuine message of my Christian parents from the beginning. I have never met any two people who embraced the gospel of Christ more than my father and mother. But entering my adolescent years, I quietly began to question whether their claims of faith were any more valid than their earlier assurances that there really was a Santa Claus.

Of course, I instinctively knew that the Santa Claus tale was meant to be childhood fun, but I also knew that belief in God the Father, Son, and Holy Ghost was serious business in our home. My parents reinforced their dedication to that belief every day of my life, and their earnest hope was that I would grow in the same tradition of faith. But by the time I was fifteen years of age, I realized that I only had one life to live and I didn't want to commit it to something I neither enjoyed nor believed.

That's not to say that I was a young atheist. My problem was with the uncertainty of it all. I didn't want to be an agnostic, but how on earth could anyone conclude whether there was an invisible God, creating and managing all life on earth and throughout the entire universe? Was I supposed to take my parents word for that? Was there a preacher, scientist, or university professor who could accurately define and confirm the existence of this higher power? If so, how?

I soon realized that I faced a monumental challenge. Now, the question before me was: What is truth? And embedded within that universal dilemma was the *real* conundrum: Is there a God? I knew that the answer to this question should become the foundation for my life's direction. But with only one life to live, would I find the answer in time? Where would I begin? And, most importantly, was I ready to accept the answer if it was ever obtainable?

Questions surrounding my life's purpose began to persist, even nag like a small inquisitive child, while the world was changing around me. The mid-'60s had arrived and the *British invasion* of America was in full swing. The artists and musicians of Europe had a flair all their own and they were overwhelming pop culture in the U.S. Everything flowing out of England was embraced by American youth with open arms. It was all innocent enough at first, but within a few short years, past counter-culture ideals came to the surface of mainstream society and, to my parent's chagrin, America was being redefined. As a young teenager, I found a lot of this cultural revolution business to be pretty exciting. The music, the styles, the art, and an ever-increasing expression of freedom were far more interesting than sitting in church and feeling admonished about the myriad things that would damn my soul for eternity. But the universal question of truth remained inside me, and I wondered if there really was something greater than myself to live for.

It didn't take long for me to become disillusioned. I would just have to go out into the world and hope that life would somehow give up the answers to its own universal questions. I decided to chart my own path and take my thoughts, interpretations, and experiences into my own hands. Adulthood would have to begin on *my* terms.

CHAPTER TWO

The Problem With Truth

To ask *what is truth?* is to ask the ultimate question, because it represents the banner under which all other questions reside. Simply stated, truth is the body of real things, events, and facts. In its totality, truth defines the past, clarifies the present, and charts the future. Ironically, nearly everyone stakes their own claim to truth in life, regardless of their background, social status, or moral view. Certainly, no one wants to declare that they live a lie, but truth poses a significant three-way problem when a person sets out to define their own worldview and direction in life.

From a human perspective, we face an initial problem in the fact that truth must first be known on an intellectual level. For such knowledge to occur, one must gain access to vast and reliable sources of information while having the ability to accurately understand it. Of course, a person would feel overwhelmed in attempting to comprehend life's full body of knowledge.

Even so, knowledge is only the first portion of the truth equation; the second concerns wisdom. Without the proper discernment that wisdom provides, our accumulated knowledge would mean little more than raw data. Wisdom is the great administrator of knowledge. Unfortunately, this essential partnership between the two is beginning to unravel in the twenty-first century as wisdom and knowledge are becoming more *inversely* proportional to each other. While knowledge is increasing at an alarming rate, wisdom is in rapid decline.

Truth also presents a third and more personal problem. It's been said that *ignorance is bliss*, and although everyone instinctively regards this as a tongue-in-cheek expression, many people are quite comfortable living by its mantra. Universal truth is comprehensive and extends to all entities in life; however, its consequences often lag in time and don't materialize right away. So, the realities that follow truth aren't always immediately recognized and it becomes easier to abide in ignorant bliss during reality's substantive dormancy. Let's face it, truth can be a tough taskmaster. Disarming truth through willful ignorance is much more convenient—for a time.

President John F. Kennedy was quoted as saying, "Too often . . . we enjoy the comfort of opinion without the discomfort of thought." For this reason, we're inclined to hold truth at bay, and neuter it so that it doesn't threaten our perceived well-being. Under such restraint, our comfort zones are no longer vulnerable territories, and our primary human concern for repose and gratification can be validated through our personal biases. After all, why should we be denied the full justification for living life on our own terms?

The problems that truth imposes don't *really* become a conscious issue with most of us until we approach the first question residing under its banner: Is there a God? Many have said that this is the most important question in life because it overshadows the significance of all other wonders and opens the door to the idea of eternal life. I would also argue that the question of God's existence is perhaps the most inescapable question of all, because if a man were to say in his heart, "I choose not to address the issue of God in my life," he would have answered the question by default, essentially taking the position of an atheist without making any effort to pursue an intellectually honest conclusion. So, the *God question* is one that cannot be ignored. It must be answered—if not by the mind, then certainly by the heart.

And so it is, that in order for us to seek God in the hope of confirming His existence, we must initially resolve the issue of intellectual honesty. This can only be done by deciding whether we're willing to leave our intellectual and emotional comfort zones to traverse the path to God's reality, wherever it might lead. This is a scary proposition, because it brings us to what can arguably be called life's greatest crossroad, located at the intersection of the secular and religious worldviews. The decision made at this point will set the foundation for all future decisions in our lives. Regretfully, we live in a world where there are more people willing to defend a lie rather than defend the truth, because blissful ignorance resides in falsehood. We'll expand on this issue in the chapter on *The Perpetual Force*.

> "When dealing with people, remember you are not dealing with creatures of logic, but with creatures of emotion, creatures bristling with prejudice and motivated by pride and vanity."
> – DALE CARNEGIE

Those who love truth, and cannot see themselves living without it, will ultimately discover truth. A personal commitment to pursue authenticity is most often motivated by the understanding that ignorant bliss is, at best, only good until reality arrives on the scene and spoils the party. And although the spoken truth doesn't always overcome a lie in the court of public opinion—or in a court of law for that matter—reality will ultimately trump a lie by imposing its consequences upon it, and thereby exposing it for the fraud that it is.

No greater example of ignorant bliss, followed by the revelation of truth, is seen than in Great Britain's delusion during the late 1930s. In his speech to British citizens, Prime Minister Neville Chamberlain declared, "peace for our time,"[1] after returning from his meeting with French government leaders and the German Führer, Adolf Hitler. But the euphoria of peace was short-lived as the truth about Hitler became known. Consequently, the world entered into an unprecedented time of war.

IN SEARCH OF DIVINE TRUTH

Self-discipline, objectivity, and sincerity are essential qualities in seeking truth and the knowledge of God. One must embrace intellectual honesty and be predetermined to avoid deception through the manipulation of facts whenever they tend to counter selfish interests. Such misrepresentation plays to our human instinct to live within our perceived comfort zones and thereby avoid the demands that truth places on us. Insincerity leads to deception. On the other hand, intellectual honesty rejects excuses for not diligently pursuing truth, and the God (if He exists) of that truth. Any compromise in this area requires an immediate resolve to get back on track and remain objective. In order to seek truth, one must be truthful. Without this purpose, there would be little value in seeking the knowledge of God. Nevertheless, neither sincerity nor intellectual honesty can stand alone in yielding the answer to life's universal question of truth. The seeker must know where to start seeking.

It's hard to tell how many different ways there are to begin the search for universal truth, but the methodologies for doing so can vary far and wide. Author Lee Strobel was an award-winning journalist at the *Chicago Tribune*, and an outspoken atheist. Lee was certain that the evidence supporting his objections to the divine were obvious and plentiful; therefore, God could not exist. In fact, he thought the idea of a living God was so absurd that its possibility really wasn't worth considering.

---

1   On September 30, 1938, Neville Chamberlain announced "peace for our time" on the steps of 10 Downing Street after returning from his trip to Munich, Germany.

In time, his wife, Leslie, became a born-again believer in Jesus Christ and Lee began to notice significant changes in her life. A loving peace began to emerge from within Leslie, but Lee was afraid that his wife would become a "religious prude" and this threatened his idea of how they should live their lives as a family. Leslie's born-again experience was intruding into Lee's comfort zone. But eventually Leslie convinced her husband to attend a church service with her, and Lee heard a sermon about the basic principles of the Christian faith. He later admitted to having some misconceptions about Christianity, but he remained an atheist.

From that point, Lee began an extensive investigation, looking for credible evidence that would either confirm the existence of God or disprove it once and for all. Although he intended to reinforce his atheistic worldview, Lee had purposed in his heart to accept the facts on their own terms. He would not seek to manipulate the information he encountered. His search included many pointed questions about Jesus of Nazareth. Was he really God's Son who died for the sins of humanity?

Lee's journey lasted almost two years and it not only took him to numerous seminary scholars, but also to sources beyond the clergy and outside the biblical record. In the end, Lee listed all the evidence for and against the existence of God and his son, Jesus Christ, and concluded that it required much more faith to remain an atheist than to receive Christ as his personal savior. Lee's life was forever changed, and from this journey came his inspired bestselling book: *The Case for Christ: A Journalist's Personal Investigation of the Evidence for Jesus*.

Another truth seeker was a young boy named Hugh Ross. Hugh grew up in the splendor of Canada's wildlife and his curiosity about life began at age seven when he went to the library to research why stars were hot. At seventeen, he became the youngest director for Vancouver's Royal Astronomical Society. After earning an undergraduate degree in physics at the University of British Columbia, he received graduate degrees in astronomy at the University of Toronto.

Dr. Hugh Ross became an astronomer, a best-selling author, and leading scholar in both apologetics and science. His book,[2] *Origins of Life*, begins with the exploration into the heart of the evolutionary argument: abiogenesis—the birth of life from non-life. Most of us are more familiar with the expression, *spontaneous generation*, to describe the same thing. But calculating the odds of such an event through natural means is impossible. According to Dr. Ross, evolution must stand on blind faith if there is no scientific evidence for the occurrence of abiogenesis, or the beginning of life without the influence of intelligent design.

> The ultimate purpose is to discover the truth.
> — ORIGINS OF LIFE

I share the stories of Dr. Ross and Lee Strobel to illustrate how one man's quest for truth can be very different from another. Strobel applied investigative journalism to answer life's universal question while Dr. Ross pursued scientific evidence and came to the same conclusion.

In great contrast, my search for truth had nothing in common with either of these educated men, and my methodology was not nearly as sophisticated. In fact, I was much too immature, naïve, and confused to take on a disciplined challenge for seeking answers to life's big questions. Besides that, I hardly knew where to begin.

In 1963, four musicians from Liverpool, England were introduced into America's pop culture. They called themselves the Beatles, and their sound, style, and long hair would quickly become a harbinger for a new ideal in

---

2   Hugh Ross co-authored *Origins of Life* with Dr. Fazale Rana, a friend and colleague who studied biochemistry at Ohio University.

much of Western society. In November of that same year, Lee Harvey Oswald assassinated President John F. Kennedy in Dallas, Texas. During that period, I was an adolescent living at home under the rule of my devoutly Christian father and mother. In the previous decade, our family's move from Atlanta to Detroit was because of my father's work, and from the beginning, my parents sought to shield me from "the ways of the world". They would have likely had greater success in that effort if we had moved to a Hutterite colony in rural Saskatchewan. But what I was learning on the streets of Motown during the mid-sixties was the antithesis of everything my parents hoped to teach me at home.

> Train up a child in the way he should go: and when he is old, he will not depart from it.
> – PROVERBS 22:6

When I turned twenty years old, the cultural revolution that began in the sixties had left an indelible mark on American society. Many of my peers in the baby-boom generation were questioning authority at every level, and in the midst of all the social noise was a proclamation that God was dead. It was a confusing time. The popular idea that everyone could (and should) *do their own thing* sounded very appealing to me at that age; yet something about this free-styled approach to life seemed too open-ended, unworkable, and at times, illogical. Nevertheless, I didn't have a definitive reason for living my life on anyone's terms but my own. This took me full circle to the back-burner questions that had been following me from the beginning: What is truth, and is there a God?

> Vanity of vanities . . . all is vanity.
> – ECCLESIASTES 12:8

I continued living my life in the hope that ultimate truth would somehow reveal itself to me in a natural way. The belief that truth resided within all of us was another popular notion of the time, but I never thought to ask how a person could extrapolate such truth from within himself. If truth was embedded within our atoms, molecules, cells, and tissues, why would the human end-product struggle with the universal questions of life? Was man not the sum of all his cells and tissues? And yet, here I was, wandering, lost, and confused in a world of unknowns.

In 1976, I had been married for three years. Shortly after the birth of our daughter, Joselyn, I moved my family to the state of Montana. I previously had been stationed in Great Falls while serving in the Air Force,[3] after returning from Vietnam in 1970. During active duty, I fell in love with America's great northwest and wanted to live in that part of the country.

A state affectionately known as *big sky country* creates many wistful expectations. Soon after relocating my family, I had an underlying hope that a new life under Montana's big sky would fulfill my sense of well-being. Unfortunately, that sense continued to remain elusive and undefined. In time, my basal hope for something to believe in had diminished and I entered into my own private despair. It had become apparent to me that I could never acquire enough knowledge during my lifetime to conclusively know whether there was anything or anyone greater than me to govern my life. Somehow, *doing my own thing* had lost much of its appeal because it provided no ultimate purpose for my existence; and I needed that purpose.

> "A man travels the world in search of what he needs and returns home to find it."
>
> – GEORGE MOORE, *THE BROOK KERITH*

---

3   Honorably discharged in August, 1973

In 1978, my family was growing with the addition of our son, Gabriel. One Sunday morning I sat in a local Baptist church, motivated only by a willingness to expose my children to some degree of Christian teaching, just as I had been at their age. They, in turn, would have to decide for themselves what worldview to embrace as they grew older. I sincerely hoped that they would have better luck than their dad was having in this area.

The church service closed with its traditional altar call, where everyone in the congregation bowed their heads in a few moments of silence. This was a time of soul-searching and reflection. Anyone ready to accept Jesus Christ as Savior into his or her life could come forward and kneel at the altar. At that point, an assigned church elder would pray the *sinner's prayer* and lead the person in repentance to salvation. I had seen this ritual countless times since childhood and yet it remained so foreign to me. With only one life to live, there was simply no way that I was going to humiliate myself in such a public display of show-and-tell. Until I knew the truth, my rear-end would remain firmly planted in that pew.

But what if there really was a God, and He really had a son who came to earth to be a sacrifice for the salvation of mankind? At that moment, it became obvious to me that I would only accept such a truth from the source—God himself. All other authorities had been disqualified. I discreetly bowed my head, closed my eyes, and quietly prayed. I laid it all on the line and told God that I didn't know whether His name was Buddha, Mohammed, or Jesus—or if He even existed at all. Nevertheless, if He was real and willing to reveal Himself to me, I was prepared to follow His truth wherever it would take me. That was the first time that I had purposed such a commitment in my search, and it was a prayer that I had never before prayed. It all left me with a strange feeling that I couldn't fully explain.

I remember walking out of the church that morning with my family and not saying a word about my experience. There had been no scientific research or journalistic investigation in my life; only the prayerful equivalent of a hail-Mary football pass to God. It was the bottom of the fourth quarter with time running out, and I had just thrown for the end zone. Suddenly there was the sobering realization that I had just made my final attempt to discover the truth of God and life itself. If He didn't somehow respond to my silent plea for help, then I knew that I would have to chart my own path for the future. There were no further options available to me.

> Ask, and it shall be given you; seek, and ye shall find; knock, and it shall be opened unto you.
>
> – MATTHEW 7:7

In the days that followed, I wondered just how God went about answering prayer—if, in fact, He answered at all. Without any intended malice, I was well beyond the point of accepting another man's opinion or testimony of God's existence. Confusion had exhausted me and I just knew that any revelation of truth would have to be very real to me. Would I actually experience a divine epiphany at a personal level? This was a tall order on my part, because I had just requested—*insisted!*—that a supernatural event take place in my life. If it were not for the fact that I was feeling a growing need for meaning and purpose, I would have never entertained such a thing. Nevertheless, it was that very need that caused me to bring full sincerity to my prayer and I meant every word of it. I was prepared to go where truth led me.

Roughly three weeks had passed since that Sunday morning and I was traveling alone on a business road trip across the great Montana landscape. Some time after settling into my 250-mile journey, God suddenly spoke to my heart in a very real way. In fact, it was so profound that my entire mind and body felt His presence. This encounter was not like anything I had previously experienced, and I knew that it was not from any figment of my imagination. I never would have thought to generate such an incident through some self-induced hyperbole. God made His presence known and told me that I would need to lean on Him in the days ahead. It was truly an emotional experience, but it resonated throughout every part of my being. It's a wonder that I didn't lose control of my vehicle.

That evening, I found a Bible and randomly opened it to the New Testament book of James. My eyes landed squarely on chapter 4, verse 13, and I began to read:

> Come now, you who say, 'Today or tomorrow we will go to such and such a city, spend a year there, buy and sell, and make a profit' . . . you do not know what will happen tomorrow. For what is your life? It is even a vapor that appears for a little time and then vanishes away.

In those short verses I saw my entire life up to that point, and I knew that God had just used His written word to put everything about me into grand perspective. An overwhelming sensation swept over me. It was the revelation of truth!

I didn't know it at the time, but I was about to experience a very difficult period in my life. Over the next three years, I went through a divorce, a job loss, and a business failure. In fact, I had my first recognizable encounter with the truth of God on that road trip and it took me entirely out of my comfort zone, but it also took me into a region that revealed the power and glory of something far greater than me. In time, God healed all of those areas of loss and went on to bless my life in so many ways.

> . . . For I neither received it from man, nor was I taught it, but it came through the revelation of Jesus Christ.
> — GALATIANS 1:12 (KJV)

The purpose for sharing my encounter with God is not to convince anyone that this really happened. With all due respect, I really don't care whether anyone believes it. The message of my testimony is simple and direct: If anyone seeks God with a sincere heart, He will make Himself known. The apostle Paul confirms this when he warns the Ephesians not to walk in the darkness of unbelieving Gentiles. They were "alienated from the life of God through their ignorance" – not intellectual ignorance, but through "the blindness of their hearts" (Ephesians 4:17, 18). God meets individuals where they live. No one has to be a scientist or an investigative reporter, or anything else, just sincere and ready to commit to the truth when it's revealed by God. It's that simple!

> And ye shall know the truth, and the truth shall make you free.
> – JOHN 8:32

EMANCIPATION THROUGH TRUTH

Many Christians miss an important point in Christ's words from John 8:32 by proclaiming that "The truth will make you free". That has become a common misquote both inside and outside the church. Through closer examination of the Scripture, we see that Jesus is essentially saying something more profound: The truth that a person *knows* is the truth that will set him free. In other words, truth is not a standalone, or stagnant solution that just happens to radiate awareness on passersby. Likewise, it isn't a serum that liberates us while residing in a bottle; rather, truth must be revealed and consumed by the individual. We must be compliant, seeking truth, accepting it, embracing it, and doing our best to live by it. In so doing, we can fully realize the real freedom of God.

TRUTH IS A PARADOX

At the beginning of this chapter, I pointed out that everyone wants to believe that he or she lives by a standard of truth; therefore, their actions and worldview are validated through that assumed reality. But *genuine* truth is an odd fellow. Time after time, it reveals itself in a paradoxical way, and that's part of the reason why truth often takes us out of our comfort zones.

What exactly is meant by saying that truth is a paradox? First, we need to understand that a paradox is something that seems contradictory and perhaps unbelievable. However, closer examination may show it to be very consistent and authentic. An example of paradox can be seen in Hegel's declaration, "We learn from history that we do not learn from history."[4] Another example can be seen in the belief that lowering taxes is more effective than raising taxes for bringing larger sums of money to government coffers. This paradox will likely play out in public debate to the end of either time or politics—whichever comes first.

When it comes to understanding the paradox through life's universal questions, the words of Jesus provide us with a good place to start. Consider Christ's words as He preached in the cities: "For my yoke is easy, and my burden is light" (Matthew 11:30). Jesus was telling everyone that they would "find rest" in their souls if they would follow Him. But in the previous chapter, Jesus states: "Think not that I am come to send peace on earth: I came not to send peace, but a sword" (Mt 10:34, KJV). It is this sword that causes strife between friends and family members. So, how do we reconcile this apparent contradiction between the images of the easy yoke and the sword?

In order to answer that question, it's important for us to understand that the *perceived* conflict with truth lies within the *real* conflict between God and Satan. Jesus never intended to "set a man at variance against his father" or anyone else, but once an individual takes a stand for truth through Christ, he will be rejected by others—including possibly members of his own family. Jesus is telling us that although His yoke is easy and His burden is light, it may (and probably will) cause others to reject us. This is an inescapable

---

4 Paraphrased from a quotation of Georg Wilhelm Friedrich Hegel.

reality in life because of sin in the world. So, this reality leads us to the paradoxical plan of redemption, which is to say that salvation is free through Christ, but it may cost us everything.

Is it any wonder that these mysteries cannot be understood by man until they're revealed by God?

> Therefore I take pleasure in infirmities, in reproaches, in necessities, in persecutions, in distresses for Christ's sake: for when I am weak, then am I strong.
> – II Corinthians 12:10

Christians, maturing in their faith, grow in the knowledge of truth and experience the joy and freedom of serving Christ throughout the many circumstances of life. They have discovered—paradoxically—that joy is often found outside of their own comfort zones.

Take the apostle Paul for example:

> *For though I be free from all men, yet have I made myself servant unto all, that I might gain the more.*
> I Corinthians 9:19, (KJV)

Paul went on to say that he became weak for the weak, and all things to all men for the cause of Christ. This was the apostle's passion and he couldn't see himself being anything else. This remains true for those committed believers today who have discovered the reality of living in the truth of God. For them, nothing else will suffice.

CHAPTER THREE

The God Who Is

> But without faith it is impossible to please Him, for he who comes to God must believe that He is...
>
> – Hebrews 11:6 (KJV)

After spending so many years in my vain attempt to answer the universal question of truth, I was amazed to discover that it is God who provides the answer at a personal level. In fact, I was never destined to rely on my own limited knowledge and experience to comprehend the living God, but that revelation was always there for the asking.

Why didn't I think of that sooner?

As the Lord declared Himself to me, I knew that I needed to pursue an understanding of my relationship to this God *who is*. It only made sense. The idea of acknowledging the reality of God, yet not seeking any further connection with Him, seemed absurd on the face of it. Fortunately, the truth of the Bible began to resonate with me the more I read it. But after going back and formally accepting Christ as my Savior at the church altar, I made a wrong assumption: I thought that I had been perfected through my faith and would never sin again. I had crossed the finish line, so to speak. After all, Jesus saved me from my sins, and I certainly didn't want to sin anymore; so that settled that. However, it wasn't long before I began to realize a new truth. First of all, I had not crossed any finish line in my spiritual life; instead, I had just taken my first step off the starting line. Secondly, my capacity to sin remained alive and well. I was reminded of that reality with every temptation that followed. I was born again, but it became apparent that this renewed life had its own unforeseen challenges.

Something didn't seem quite right in my newfound faith. How could Jesus save me from my sins, cleanse me from all unrighteousness, and give me a desire to live a perfect life through His Spirit, while the carnal emotions of my inner being continued to rise up and contradict the revelation of God? I began to feel a sense of discouragement, and wondered whether I was just fooling myself in this search for truth.

One evening, I was reading in the book of Romans and came upon chapter seven. Its author, the apostle Paul, began by addressing matters of marriage, adultery, and divorce. He then moved to the subject of God's law and began to expound on how that law affects the relationship between God and man. As Paul's description unfolded, my spirit was revitalized. Paul became very transparent as he revealed the details of his own personal struggle with the very law that he praised. I realized that Paul had undergone the same dichotomy that I was experiencing. His inner man was "warring" against the law of God, and he didn't like it any better than I did.

> For we know that the law is Spiritual, but I am carnal, sold under sin. For what I am doing, I do not understand. For what I will to do, that I do not practice; but what I hate, that I do. If, then, I do what I will not to do, I agree with the law that *it is* good. But now, *it is* no longer I who do it, but sin that dwells in me. For I know that in me (that is, in my flesh) nothing good dwells; for to will is present with me, but *how* to perform what is good I do not find. For the good that I will *to do,* I do not do; but the evil I will not *to do,* that I practice. Now if I do what I will not *to do,* it is no longer I who do it, but sin that dwells in me. I find then a law, that evil is present with me, the one who wills to do good. For I delight in the law of God according to the inward man. But I see another law in my members, warring against the law of my mind, and bringing me into captivity to the law of sin which is in my members. O wretched man that I am! Who will deliver me from this body of death?
> — ROMANS 7:14-24 (NASB)

In chapter 7, verses 25 through chapter 8:1, Paul reveals the solution to the conflict:

> *I thank God—through Jesus Christ our Lord! So then, with the mind I myself serve the law of God, but with the flesh the law of sin. There is therefore now no condemnation to those who are in Christ Jesus, who do not walk according to the flesh, but according to the Spirit.*

Paul had just provided a grand overview of the Christian experience by revealing a divine paradox: Although the Christian is saved from sin, he is still subject to sin because of its persistence through man's carnal nature. In reality, we're all packaged in the fallen state of the flesh—a state of sin.

In order to honor God in this dichotomy, the Christian consciously partners with Christ in a love relationship through His Holy Spirit and is thereby set free from all condemnation.

This amazing, yet misunderstood, relationship helps explain why many non-believers reject the gospel of Christ, and the Christian life altogether. The natural man tends to seek alternatives to enduring conflicts between flesh and spirit by assuming goodness through his own autonomy. As mentioned in the chapter on Truth, human nature seeks to stay within the comfort zone of its own worldview. In so doing, the mind formulates an intellectual justification for the heart's rejection of God in order to set the conscience free. Ask those of a secular bent to expound on their views of life and death, and you will likely hear a wide variety of customized explanations, made-to-order for each individual.

On the other hand, people who follow after the ways of God and seek to live according to the Bible build their faith on its standards and instruction. As previously illustrated, this certainly doesn't make them perfect human beings. Christians, like everyone, are born with different personalities, talents and weaknesses; so God is not expecting His followers to be perfect or exact copies of one another. However, when the biblical foundation of love defines the relationship between believers and God's spirit, the Christian voice becomes unified in its message to an unbelieving world. This process describes the great commission that Christ has placed on His church: to love one another and preach the gospel throughout the world (Mark 16:15). And though each dedicated follower of Christ experiences conflicts between flesh and spirit, they are keenly aware that a relationship with God puts into motion an adventurous journey and a victorious life.

> What then shall we say to these things? If God is for us, who can be against us?
>
> – ROMANS 8:31 (NKJV)

GOD'S PARADIGM

Over the years, popular fads have come and gone; everything from ant farms to mood rings to break dancing. Fads have played some part in social life throughout most—if not all—of civilization. Christians have fads too. As you might expect, they're attached to some divine meaning and are often expressed in a propitious way. I refer to them as fads because, although they're well-intended, they have a tendency to go out of fashion over time. One such example can be seen at a large gathering of Christians at a major rally or musical event. The event might be held in a stadium or large auditorium. Before the program starts, a section of people will stand to their feet and chant, "We love Jesus, yes we do. We love Jesus, how about you?" The idea of this exercise is to encourage people from another section of the stadium to stand, repeat the chant, and verbally "pass it" over to yet another section in the audience.

Another popular Christian fad doesn't involve any vocal expression, but is generally displayed on a car's bumper sticker, or on articles of clothing. It reads *NOTW*, in gothic styled fonts, and means "not of this world." The abbreviation is intended to announce that the individual has placed his or her affections in the heavenly things of God rather than in the temporal things of earth.

There was one fad that tended to capture my imagination. Like the NOTW logo, this popular Christian expression involved an abbreviation. It read: WWJD (*What would Jesus do?*) Interestingly, the secular media would sometimes modify this popular abbreviation and apply it to a celebrity or public official, in some humorous manner. But the original intent of WWJD was to ask the individual to stop and consider what Jesus would do in their present situation at any given moment in time.

After taking that challenge and attempting to apply the WWJD rule to my own daily living, I soon became confounded. There were so many variables in life and I found it perplexing trying to figure out what Jesus would do for every event, action, and spoken word throughout my daily affairs. Would Jesus ever drive 51 mph in a 50 mph zone? How would He vote on a jury that involved a mandatory death sentence? And to what extent would Jesus argue a procedural point in a corporate board meeting? The questions are endless and it was obvious to me that there was no quick fix to resolving all of life's conflicts based on WWJD.

> Consider what I say, for the Lord will give you understanding in everything.
>
> – II Timothy 2:7 (KJV)

Before attempting to understand what Jesus would do in any given situation, we must first *see* what Jesus sees. In other words, we must view the situation or person through His looking glass if we ever hope to make a correct assessment and proceed with Christ's response. This change in perspective is often referred to as a *paradigm shift*. In Romans 12:2, the apostle Paul calls it a *"renewing of your mind"*. Such a perceptual transformation is more than just a cerebral experience, it's the result of God's Spirit influencing the worldview and daily thought processes of believers who continually seek wisdom.

The activity of renewing one's mind is not something that occurs in an instant; rather, it's a lifelong progression that matures over time. The paradigm shift towards a godly worldview grows incrementally, and increasingly gives the spiritual man the upper hand in the daily dichotomy of Romans 7. No longer does the believer list the same priorities or judge others in the same way, because everything begins to look a lot different through God's looking glass. As a result, the believer develops a greater capacity to grow in faith, and benefit from an ordered life that is blessed by God. Beyond that, the believer experiences a natural compassion—or more accurately, a supernatural compassion—for others and seeks to share the blessings and truths that the believer himself has experienced. Life takes on a new look and feel.

> Turn your eyes upon Jesus, look full in His wonderful face; and the things of earth will grow strangely dim in the light of His glory and grace.
> – Turn Your Eyes Upon Jesus
> hymn by Helen H. Lemmel

The importance of seeing things through God's looking glass cannot be overstated. It's essential to personal spiritual growth and our ability to effectively witness the reality of Christ to a lost world.

JUDGMENT AND CONDEMNATION

People may say that they can't worship a God who seems as cruel as the one described in the Old Testament. When confronted with this complaint, many Christians don't quite know how to respond, because they themselves have struggled with this very issue.

> The young and the old lie on the ground in the streets:
> My virgins and my young men are fallen by the sword;
> Thou hast slain them in the day of thine anger; thou hast killed, and not pitied.
> – Lamentations 2:21

Time and again the Bible reveals the judgment of the Lord. In our normal thinking, we imagine that God, like President Harry Truman, should have a plaque on His grand mahogany desk that reads: *The buck REALLY stops here!*

If God is the omnipotent One, why has He not applied a more tempered way to deal with the shortcomings of humanity throughout the course of history? After all, the best-known Scripture in the Bible tells us that *"God so loved the world..."* (John 3:16). How then, do we reconcile this apparent contradiction? Without seeing the truth of sin and its universal impact on mankind, we can't begin to comprehend the divine rationale behind the harsh events of the Old Testament and still see a loving God in the midst of it all.

Perhaps a good place to begin in this understanding is by answering the question: What makes a meaningful relationship? Beyond love, most of us would agree that hope, sincerity, trust, adventure, volition, temptation and consequence would be among the essential elements that would define the value of an intimate bond. This is certainly true in the accord between God and man.

The author John Steinbeck alludes to this theme in a scene from his classic novel, *The Log from the Sea of Cortez (1951)*. In this instance, Steinbeck's "relational reality" involves a fish and a fisherman under two different circumstances.

> *For example, the Mexican sierra has 'XVII-15-IX' spines in the dorsal fin. These can be easily counted. But if the sierra strikes hard on the line so that our hands are burned, if the fish sounds and nearly escapes and finally comes in over the rail, his colors pulsing and his tail beating the air, a whole new relational externality has come into being – an entity which is more than the sum of the fish plus the fisherman.*

> *The only way to count the spines of the sierra unaffected by this second relational reality is to sit in a laboratory, open an evil-smelling jar, remove a stiff colorless fish from formalin solution, count the spines, and write the truth 'D.XVII-15-IX.' There you have recorded a reality which cannot be assailed – probably the least important reality concerning either the fish or yourself.*

If there is any analogy to be found in Steinbeck's fish, we may see ourselves "beating the air" with "colors pulsing" as God reaches out to us. So much is at risk as we fight against God's law of righteousness through our own preconceived notions of His ultimate intent. This defines sin at each individual level, and consequences emerge from the simultaneous events of our rebellious struggle and God's active plan for an eternal love relationship.

On the other hand, God could have simply created us with biological programming and all the necessary parts to passively do His will forever and ever. There would be no purpose in questioning the origin of truth, or the reason for love. Life lessons would not exist because we would never be subjected to making a critical decision in life. And like the fish in the "evil smelling jar," we would only be suitable for cataloging.

> Where were you when I laid the foundations of the earth?
> Tell Me, if you have understanding.
> — Job 38:4 (NKJV)

It's the duty of believers everywhere to seek understanding in this area and be able to articulate the real truth of God and His perspective in this cosmic battle of good and evil. Sin has devastating consequences; unfortunately, too many Christians today—leaders and laity alike—have taken a more buffered approach in dealing with sin, thinking that they might somehow offend or scare those who disregard the existence of a living God. Over time, sin can seem increasingly benign to both Christians and nonbelievers, while God's divine judgment appears more unfair. As a result, the Lord's love and mercy towards humankind is lost in the debate because the apparent cruelty of the Old Testament God remains unjustified in the minds of many people. Eventually, God becomes the culprit and believers fail to defend His character with the testimony of their words and deeds.

THE PERSONAL GOD

> You believe that there is one God.
> Good for you. Even the demons believe—and tremble.
> – JAMES 2:19 (PARAPHRASED)

In order to obtain a deeper understanding of the God *who is*, we must move beyond a superficial "belief" and seek a personalized relationship with our Creator. The disciple Mark records the final hours of Christ during His agony in the garden of Gethsemane. In Mark 14:36, Jesus reveals the very real association that He has with the heavenly Father by calling Him, *"Abba, Father"*. The word *Abba* is an Aramaic expression used to describe Father in an intimate and respectful sense. In like manner, the apostle Paul reveals to believers that *". . . because you are sons, God hath sent forth the Spirit of his Son into your hearts, crying, Abba, Father,"* (Galatians 4:6). And in Romans 8:15, Paul states that God's Spirit receives us into adoption rather than bondage. As a result, our relationship to the Father is as sons and daughters *"whereby we cry, Abba, Father."*

This declaration personalizes our relationship to our Creator in a way that is unfathomable through a secular worldview. But this heavenly relationship is not merely a one-sided affair. We, as Christians, can easily undermine this intimate alliance through disobedience and compromise. Considering Jesus in the garden of Gethsemane, we see that during the dark hours before His execution, Christ remained steadfast in obedience to the Father by stating, *". . . nevertheless, not my will, but Thine be done,"* (Mark 14:32). In so doing, Jesus put into motion the Father's perfect will and the future of the entire human race for all eternity.

So, the name *Abba* not only asserts a personal and spiritually intimate relationship to our heavenly Father, it also makes a useful acronym that helps identify important steps that believers should take in order to partner in a loving relationship through the Holy Spirit, and know God in the most personal way:

A = Ask: As previously stated, we must ask God to enable us to view people and events as He views them; continually seeking the paradigm of Christ and seeing life through His looking glass rather than our own. Seeking God for His worldview is done through the study of His word and continual prayer with diligence—not allowing complacency to undermine this effort. This lifelong quest is simply a matter of seeking wisdom, and it's vital to personal growth and meaningful relationship with God.

B = Bible: In short, read it! Regardless of how many church services, Bible studies, seminars, or workshops a Christian attends, there's no substitute for prayerfully meditating on God's word when no one else is around. It's the most direct way that He communicates with us on a personal level. This is where real transformation takes place and it's essential to our love relationship with God and with people around us. All other Christian activities that we may involve ourselves with are good and purposeful, but they must be subject to the written Word in order to contribute to the development of our alliance with God.

> All scripture is given by inspiration of God, and is profitable for doctrine, for reproof, for correction, for instruction in righteousness: That the man of God may be perfect, thoroughly furnished unto all good works.
> – II Timothy 3:16-17 (KJV)

In addition to providing an avenue through which the Spirit delivers God's word to us, the Bible establishes a reliable standard for determining right from wrong, while offering insight, wisdom, hope, and confidence for all eternity. In a world that continually seeks to redefine itself, the Bible stands the test of time for ultimate truth. Hebrews 13:8 declares that *"... Christ is the same yesterday, today, and forever."*

B = Believe: Ultimately, we must be convinced that the gospel of Christ, and everything it encompasses, is true. Such recognition is realized through the personal witness of others, the sound doctrine of Scripture, and the revelations and experiences that come from prayer and the experiences of Christian living.

> So then faith comes by hearing, and hearing by the word of God.
> – Romans 10:17 (NKJV)

In his book of essays, *God in the Dock*, C.S. Lewis points out that we are not Christians because Christianity makes us feel good, or somehow comforts us through life's circumstances; rather, we are Christians because we *really* believe that Jesus went to the cross, died, and rose again for the salvation of mankind.

That's why we are Christians!

A = Apply: We act on what we believe. As the reality of God becomes more apparent, and we incrementally move deeper into His paradigm through the renewing of our minds, there emerges a greater avidity to love people, share our faith, support our church, forgive others, speak the truth, make personal sacrifices, seek the Spirit's guidance, and look for new methodologies that honor our Creator as Abba, Father, and His son, Jesus Christ.

No meaningful relationship can remain healthy without a genuine application of confirmation. That's where *works* come in. And although we are saved by grace rather than "works," our actions are an important expression of love towards our Abba, Father. After all, there are a lot of things that He hopes to accomplish through us during this lifetime, and the demonstration of our best efforts is an essential part of His eternal game plan. No one can make the argument that dormant faith makes an effective testimony that leads anyone to salvation.

> Even so faith, if it hath not works, is dead, being alone.
> – James 2:17 (KJV)

THE PRACTICAL GOD

Years ago, I worked as a journeyman lineman in the electrical industry. On one occasion, my crew foreman, Chuck, told me about something he experienced while being interviewed for the foreman position. Because of rigid company standards and procedures, it was not uncommon for a potential employee candidate to endure numerous interviews for this job. Questioning was often tough and intimidating. On his final interview, Chuck was asked, "During emergency work, how much would you allow each crew member to spend for food when the crew breaks for a meal?"

This was always a touchy issue with the company. Although there was never a defined dollar amount allotted for crew meals, management often complained when high-dollar receipts were turned in from the more expensive restaurants in the area. And they were determined to put an end to this practice.

Chuck's response caught everyone by surprise, "I'd let the crew go to any restaurant near our work location and eat all they wanted."

"Really?" one interviewer bristled.

"Yes," replied Chuck, with confidence.

He went on to explain that the union contract allowed the workers to break for a meal every four hours while working in a storm or other emergency condition. That meant that any crew member could shut down the job every four hours and demand a trip to the restaurant. Such a schedule would cripple any significant restoration effort and customer service would fall well below the company standard. By letting the crew fill up on good food at a place of their choice, no one would want to eat again for at least another six to eight hours.

After hearing Chuck's reasoning, the management staff realized that he was right and a greater purpose was being achieved through his method. It was apparent that everyone concerned—the company, the crew, and the customers—would benefit by not imposing this stern (though informal) policy in an oppressive manner. Not long afterwards, Chuck was awarded the foreman position and assigned his first truck and crew.

Chuck's experience reminds me of an occasion when Jesus was leading his disciples on the Sabbath day through a corn field. As they were partaking of the corn, Jesus was approached by a few critical Pharisees who were quick to inform Jesus that He and His *crew* of disciples were in technical violation of the policies and procedures outlined in the law. Jews were not allowed to harvest food on the day of the Sabbath, but Jesus reminded the Pharisees that King David had once eaten of the forbidden showbread in the temple because he and his men were simply hungry, and they were not found guilty before God (Mark 2:23-26). Jesus went one step further by stating, *"The Sabbath was made for man, and not man for the Sabbath. So, the Son of Man is also Lord of the Sabbath"* (vv. 27-28). This declaration laid the foundation for understanding how this law—and the entire law—was given by God to serve a greater cause than just the edict itself. Throughout their years of study, this truth had eluded the Pharisees.

Through His death and resurrection, Jesus became the perfect and ultimate sacrifice, thereby fulfilling the whole law and consolidating it into two simple mandates for humankind: First of all, love God; and secondly, love your neighbor as much as you love yourself (Matt 22:37-40). And although the *principles* of the Old Testament law are carried forward into the modern age, everything our Abba Father desires of us hangs on those two precepts of love.

How simple is that!

So, what is the problem? Why, after thousands of years, do we still struggle with the idea of living within the perfect will of God?

Why indeed.

These questions bring us to yet another paradox of truth: In his grand effort to find personal fulfillment through the easiest available means, man seeks to bypass God's *simple* path in exchange for the complex and failed methodologies of the world, and then justify it all through his own paradigm.

There is a word that captures the essence of this strange behavior. It's called *sin*.

CHAPTER FOUR

The Perpetual Force

Not long after my discharge from the Air Force in 1973, I started attending evening classes at a local technical school. My course of study was in radio electronics, and I remember a lecture the instructor gave on the subject of energy and how it could be transformed from one state to another. He asked the class to imagine an automobile with a motor that had the capacity to capture its own mechanical energy and recycle it with one hundred percent efficiency. The result would enable the car to run continually on its own reprocessed power. Such a vehicle, he said, could operate on perpetual motion and would, no doubt, make its inventor very wealthy. But any student of physics knows that creating such a machine is presently considered impossible. So far, every attempt to do so has been restricted by the scientific laws of thermodynamics. In short, these laws tell us that although we can transform energy from one state to another, we can't preserve it with one hundred percent efficiency. Energy will deplete over time unless it's resupplied from an external source.

However, there is a universal state into which we are born that continually imposes itself on humankind with devastating results. It's the state of sin, and it functions much like a perpetual ubiquitous force that shapes the course of global events, and every living thing is affected by it. There's no need to refuel this sin-born energy. Unceasingly, it coexists with all people, and neither its containment nor termination is possible through human strength alone.

Everyone suffers from the consequences of sin, but nonbelievers don't readily make the connection between their rejection of God and the results that follow. The secular worldview doesn't give place to such an interpretation. But unbelievers aren't the only ones who fall short when it comes to seeing sin for what it really is. A number of people proclaiming to be Christians express doubt that the Bible remains fully relevant in a twenty-first century world. Applying biblical principles to daily life is becoming uncommon and the idea of being a *holy people* is less popular than ever before in America. Today, we often abuse the sole principle of being *saved by grace* to carelessly exercise our "freedoms" and thereby undermine personal spiritual growth. As previously noted, human nature seeks to reside within its own comfort zone. But believers who leverage God's grace, and excuse themselves from a holy and obedient lifestyle, undermine the most important relationship of their lives and enter vulnerable territories.

> I will set nothing wicked before my eyes…
> – Psalm 101:3 (NKJV)

The problem is, our supposed freedoms are often reflected through the works of compromises that involve some form of vice. Keep in mind that a presumptive accusation is not being expressed here. After all, if a believer views a movie or program that tends to glorify sex and violence, that doesn't mean that he or she will go out and act on those principles. But by now, it should be obvious to Christians everywhere that continued exposure to such entertainment tends to desensitize the church body towards the reality of sin, and by its very nature, this desensitizing process takes place in a subtle and gradual manner. Nevertheless, this spiritual anesthetizing of the saints is a component of the perpetual force of sin that is plaguing the world.

> Finally, brethren, whatever things are true, whatever things are noble, whatever things are just, whatever things are pure, whatever things are lovely, whatever things are of good report, if there is any virtue and if there is anything praiseworthy—meditate on these things.
> – PHILIPPIANS 4:8 (NKJV)

Is it any wonder that the church is failing to impact modern culture? Too often, sermons from the pulpits across America have effectively communicated the joys of knowing Christ as Savior while keeping the subject of sin on a broader, more superficial level. And while believers acknowledge that the "wages of sin is death," a righteous indignation towards it, and a passion for holiness is clearly missing in many of today's churches. As a result, the troubles of the world have become troubles for the body of Christ: divorce, out-of-wedlock pregnancies, and pornography addiction, just to name a few. Sin undermines the opportunity that we, as believers in Christ, have to provide solutions to current problems along with the message of hope and eternal life. But if we aren't the *solution* to the problem, we'll become the *enablers* of the problem.

You can generally count on folks to throw out the proverbial baby with the bathwater. Whenever Christians violate or compromise the very truth they proclaim (whether in a major or minor way), the world is quick to reject both the message and the God of that message. Perceived hypocrisy—real or imagined—is like a bullet to the head, and it can kill our testimony in an instant. But the Lord empowers our witness if we consistently apply due diligence by first *living* the truth before bothering to proclaim it.

KNOW YOUR ENEMY

It's easy for us to become discouraged when we see the world grappling with that age old question: *Why do bad things happen to good people?* And it's not only unbelievers who are challenged with this thought; we all carry the burden of this question. God's people must prayerfully seek a deeper understanding of the full nature of sin and how it functions in both the individual's life and throughout an entire social system.

> And the Lord said unto Satan, "The Lord rebuke thee, O Satan!"
> – Zechariah 31:2 (KJV)

Satan is the perfect storm, an all-inclusive enemy, and a powerful desperado. He brings all the elements of destruction to fight a war that he has already lost—and he knows it. But Satan's foreknowledge of his own destiny makes him more than a formidable enemy. Imagine what it must feel like knowing that your soul will be forever damned and there's nothing that you can do about it. That's Satan's dilemma. After being a part of God's kingdom, he decided to lead a host of angels in a heavenly coup and take the reins of universal power from God. But the attempted coup failed and its outcome has left Satan and his demons destined for an eternal hell.

It's beyond human comprehension to fully grasp the significance of this celestial revolution, and the Bible provides limited insight into what must have been a colossal struggle. Who can visualize a loving and omnipotent God coming under attack from within His own kingdom? Yet, this remarkable and dynamic conflict provides us with the framework for understanding all of life's struggles—even death itself.

> And [Jesus] said to them, "I was watching Satan fall from heaven like lightning."
> – Luke 10:18 (NASB)

Although we lack the details of Satan's fall from grace, it's imperative that we have a clear view of how he operates in the world today. Fortunately, God's word provides us with rich insight if we're willing to study it. In I John 3:8, we see that the devil has sinned from the very beginning of humanity. And it was in the beginning that Satan, as the serpent, confronted Eve in the garden with a plan to lure her into disobedience to God. The dialog that takes place between the two of them in Genesis chapter 3, gives us a front row seat to witness the smoothest con ever devised. In verse 1, the serpent is introduced with a character trait that is summed up in one word: *cunning*. As he approaches Eve, he asks what appears to be a benign question, "Has God indeed said, 'You shall not eat of every tree of the garden?'"

The serpent has just put the ball in Eve's court, so to speak. What occurs next will be determined by her answer, and at this point an interesting thing happens. Eve responds to the serpent's question by reciting God's command, forbidding the eating of the tree's fruit; but for some unknown reason, she inserts an additional restriction, not previously mentioned in scripture: ". . . nor shall you touch [the tree], lest you die" (Genesis 3:3). This is a very interesting response because it begs the question: Why would anyone add an additional restriction to the original mandate?

Perhaps there's a human tendency to incorporate a self-imposed buffer, designed to help prevent the violation of a law that we don't like in the first place, but it's an immature act of insecurity. Whatever Eve's reason happened to be, she ended up violating the same instruction in Genesis that God gives to everyone in the book of Revelation:

> *"For I testify to everyone who hears the words of the prophecy of this book: If anyone adds to these things, God will add to him the plagues that are written in this book; and if anyone takes away from the words of the book of this prophecy, God shall take away his part from the Book of Life, from the holy city, and from the things which are written in this book."*
>
> Revelation 22:18, 19 (KJV)

So, the instruction is clear throughout history: Do not alter the word of God! When Eve violated this command, she entered into Satan's arena.

A TRUE IMAGE DOES NOT A REALITY MAKE

Most photographers will tell you that the camera never lies. But it doesn't necessarily tell the truth either. When the shutter opens and closes, the camera captures the image that the lens sees. But in the end, the image is dependent on the interpretation of the individual viewing it. For example, an outdoor photograph of a young girl stooping over in a massive shower of water can give more than one impression. Is the girl playing in a large fountain spray, or is this a photo of a victim in the midst of a hurricane? Although the lens has presented the truth of the image, it fails to reveal its reality.

In a similar manner, the serpent deceives Eve through a series of technical truths. He begins in Genesis 3:4 by telling her that she will not die from eating the fruit of the tree. And that's true. Eve will not die—at least, not right away. But she has no way of understanding how her disobedience will make death a reality for herself, and for all future generations.

Next, Satan declares that God knows that once Eve eats of the fruit, she will then have her eyes opened and obtain a new knowledge of good and evil—just like a god! Again, Satan has spoken a truth; however, he is beyond contemptible because, like the camera lens, he has presented an image without its reality, and he knows exactly how that image is being interpreted by Eve. In verse 6, the scripture reveals Eve's analysis of the serpent's words and the attractive view of the tree that stands before her. She then eats of the fruit and shares with Adam.

The rest is history.

One can only wonder what the world would have been like if only Eve ate of the fruit and not Adam; or, if neither of them ate from the tree. We may never know, but it would be safe to say that without the cunning deception of the serpent, the consequences that followed would be greatly diminished. But as it now stands, we're faced with the reality of death along with the pain and suffering that accompanies it.

THE WORKFLOW PROCESS

For every task there's a methodology, often referred to as a workflow process. Many larger jobs tend to formalize their workflow processes through policies and procedures outlined in operation manuals, job aids or user guides. These processes generally involve steps that the worker takes at a first stage of development, then move on to the steps of a second stage, then a third, along a linear work path until the final stage has been completed. At that point, *Voila'!* A new widget is born.

> Then when lust has conceived, it gives birth to sin; and when sin is accomplished, it brings forth death.
> – James 1:15 (NASB)

As it happens, the Bible reveals that Satan and his demonic cohorts also have a defined methodology. In James 1:15 we see a three-staged workflow that consists of: (1) Lust, (2) Sin, and (3) Death. Like many workflow processes, Satan's methodology begins with its simplest step, and then moves towards greater complexity until the final stage of production is complete—in t' case, death and destruction.

So, what does this workflow look like when it's put into actio' already taken a brief look at the serpent in the garden with his plan to entice, entrap, and destroy. But let's look at another example through two separate scenarios to illustrate an important point. Our stories will involve a businessman, whom we'll name Robert. He's married with two children and lives in a nice home in the suburbs. Robert has a good job and a happy family life.

Scenario #1: Robert is traveling alone, out of state on business. At his company's convention, he meets a beautiful young lady from another department and they get into a long conversation over cocktails. One thing leads to another and the young lady ends up in Robert's hotel room where the convention is being held. The two of them have a sexual affair that same evening.

A couple of weeks go by and Robert's wife learns of the affair. She is devastated and approaches him in tears, demanding a divorce. Robert is broken with grief and pleads with his wife to give him another chance. He tells her that the affair meant nothing and promises to do anything to restore his relationship to his wife.

"I just had a weak moment," he cries.

We'll stop the story at this point and rewind to the beginning. This time, our tale will involve a slight change of events.

Scenario #2: Again, Robert is traveling out of state on business. At his company's convention, he meets a beautiful young lady from another department and they get into a long conversation. During their talk, a friend of Robert discreetly approaches and slips him a folded piece of paper. Momentarily, Robert carefully unfolds the paper and reads the words: "Her name is Michele. She is the wife of a mafia crime boss in Chicago. And she has tested ˥itive for HIV and other sexually transmitted diseases."

ᴨder both scenarios, certain questions may arise. First of all, does either present a condition whereby our friend, Robert, will somehow find it within himself to overcome his "weak moment" and not pursue an affair with the young lady? Chances are, most people would put their money on Robert in scenario #2, and bet that he would take the moral high-ground and stay true to his wife.

But why would the second example likely alter Robert's actions? What is the fundamental difference between the two scenarios?

Before jumping to a quick and obvious conclusion, let's compare the two scenes by projecting them against Satan's workflow process. Remember, the first stage of production involves lust—without which, no incentive would exist to proceed to the second stage of sin. So, in the first scenario, Robert finds himself in the midst of lust without any apparent consideration of where this encounter will take him, and that's exactly where Eve found herself in the garden with the serpent.

In the first part of Satan's workflow, everything feels good and looks good. Lust is always warm and cozy. And this period can last for an extended duration. The Bible refers to this time as "the passing pleasures of sin . . . (Hebrews 11:25). Lust represents the image before the reality, and in this case, Robert's awareness of this encounter is void of consideration for what is about to transpire after the sexual affair.

However, the second scenario is quite different. Robert's discreet friend has provided him with some valuable information. Assuming that Robert takes this information seriously, he'll now have a much clearer picture of the remaining components in Satan's workflow process. In other words, while in the midst of the lust stage, he'll envision stages two and three with remarkable clarity. Robert will know where a sexual encounter with this lady is likely to end up.

This type of human interaction takes place countless times every day. And Robert's story is only one of the many temptations that occur in human life; yet, these tragedies follow the same perpetual workflow of lust, sin, and death.

Keep in mind that the final stage of death doesn't necessarily refer to a physical end of life—although it often does. Satan uses his template to incorporate demonic forces that destroy relationships, finances, opportunities, freedom, respect, or anything of value. But the ultimate goal of Satan's final process is the death of the soul and eternal damnation. For this reason, Christians have been assigned the great duty of maintaining clarity throughout our enemy's workflow methods. Therefore, when we find ourselves in the realm of temptation (e.g., the first stage of lust), it's imperative that we see the end from the beginning, throughout Satan's entire perpetual operation.

For those who know Christ as Savior and seek to grow in wisdom, there's a friend who offers insight, and He's a greater ally than Robert's friend. He is the Holy Spirit of God who ministers to believers in time of need. The Holy Spirit serves, not only as a comforter, but also as a witness with our spirits, warning us when we're being tempted. And He strengthens us when we're being tested through various trials.

BEING LIKE GOD

Satan's workflow process also can be seen as a highway of death (which is where it ends), and this highway has a frontage road, running parallel to the same destructive end. It is the road of human autonomy.

> There is a way that seems right to a man, but its end is the way of death.
> – PROVERBS 16:25 (NKJV)

Once man obtained the knowledge of good and evil in the garden, he began to emerge with a sense of independence and self-rule. And why not? He now could decide for himself what was right and what was wrong—apart from God. There are a lot of "good" people who live their lives with this sense of autonomy. But assuming a life of secular sovereignty blinds people to the realities of sin, robbing them of the clarity that can only come through divine insight.

In a social system, this breach in relationship between man and his Creator results in a discontinuity between society and the wisdom needed for proper governance. This is especially true in the twenty-first century when knowledge has never been greater while, at the same time, wisdom continues to decline. What *then* emerges is the ageless propensity for power and control coupled with a new age of technology committed to social dominance. In time, knowledge without wisdom creates a very dangerous world.

> For the wisdom of this world is foolishness with God. For it is written, He takes the wise in their own craftiness. And again, the Lord knows the thoughts of [man], that they are vain.
> – I Corinthians 3:19-20 (KJV)

As the inversion between knowledge and wisdom increases, mankind moves ever closer to sin's final stage of death. But in the greatest of ironies, death itself becomes a necessary part of life, because it serves as a stop-gap for what would otherwise be an endless decay of every living entity. Without death, there could be no chance for renewal; no vitality, joy, peace, abundance, or an opportunity for restoration. In fact, life would not be worth living. But because of God's love for all humanity, death is conquered through Jesus Christ. As a result, believers should no longer fear death or see it as the ultimate end of life; rather, as a transition to a new and eternal life—and one without sin.

> The sting of death is sin; and the strength of sin is the law. But thanks be to God, which gives us the victory through our Lord Jesus Christ.
> – I Corinthians 15:55-57 (KJV)

The reason behind such fearlessness is the essence of John 3:16-17:

> *"For God so loved the world that He gave His only begotten Son, that whoever believes in Him should not perish but have everlasting life.*
>
> *For God did not send His Son into the world to condemn the world, but that the world through Him might be saved."*

In the global state of sin, we simply cannot fulfill the requirements of God's divine law through our own strength, charm, intellect, or good intentions. As a result, the rejection of God's plan leaves the autonomous man with no alternate means for the salvation of his soul. Scripture puts this reality into focus as we continue with John 3:18-21:

> *"The one who believes in [Christ] is not judged, but the one who does not believe has already been judged, because he has not believed in the name of the one and only Son of God. And this is the judgment: that the light has come into the world, and people loved the darkness rather than the light, because their deeds were evil. For everyone who practices evil hates the light and does not come to the light, lest his deeds be exposed. But the one who practices the truth comes to the light, in order that his deeds may be revealed, that they are done in God."*
>
> LEXHAM ENGLISH BIBLE

In the end, there can only be one conclusion: We love God because He first loved us (I John 4:19); conversely, God rejects us because we first rejected Him.

CHAPTER FIVE

The Prelude to Prayer

Early morning and a quick trip to the store, I pulled behind a pickup truck at a stop sign, its bumper sticker displaying that familiar three-word prayer; an appeal seen by millions as it's heralded across the country. It read, *God Bless America*.

Few folks might consider this short phrase to be a prayer in the traditional sense, but this simple petition contains all the essential elements of prayer by first addressing God, then entreating Him for a blessing. At the moment I read that bumper sticker, I reiterated the plea in my heart, "Yes God, please bless America!"

To my surprise, I sensed God's immediate response. "Why?" He asked.

Why? The question rolled around in my head. I had always assumed the request spoke for itself, without a need for further elaboration. But my assumption was thoughtless, and I suddenly realized that God's response was both appropriate and essential—one that demanded an answer. Why, indeed, should God continue to bless America? Do we see ourselves as "the good guys" throughout the modern world? I would like to think so, but considering the contrast between our nation's Christian heritage and its modern trend towards secularism and immorality, we must reevaluate who we really are as a nation.

Would the *good guys* pervert their hard-fought freedoms by allowing new vice industries such as pornography, prostitution, and the legalization of marijuana to define the American way of life? Would good people kill over 60 million of their unborn citizens, redefine their family structure, and use their institutions in education, the arts, and entertainment to tear down traditional Christian values?

Unfortunately, America is guilty of all this and more. Never before has there been a nation so blessed of God. And whether a blessing is bestowed on the individual citizen or all of society, the mandate is clear:

> "... *For everyone to whom much is given . . . much will be required.*"
>
> Luke 12:48 (KJV)

What seemed to be a simple three-word prayer suddenly became something much more significant. How many times have we uttered the words *God bless America* without ever considering whether our country remains worthy of such a blessing? The amazing reality is that God has never stopped blessing America. The mounting problems we currently face as a nation are overwhelmingly the result of foolish choices made by our generation. Yet, God has placed within our reach the resources and solutions to our country's major predicaments, if we'll only turn our hearts to Him in humble prayer and seek wisdom. For this reason, it's a total waste of time to blame certain traditions and events from past generations for our perceived woes—real or imagined. We are fully capable of resolving many of the problems that have, for too long, plagued America, and we have the responsibility to do so.

Perhaps the Lord would see fit to display His *own* bumper sticker in response to our national appeal. It might read: *America, Bless God!* That would represent a radical change in direction for the *good guys*.

> If my people, which are called by my name, shall humble themselves, and pray, and seek my face, and turn from their wicked ways; then will I hear from heaven, and will forgive their sin, and will heal their land.
> – II Chronicles 7:14,15 (KJV)

WHAT IS PRAYER?

At this point, it might be good to stop and ask: Exactly, what is prayer? Is it something so subjective that people must define it for themselves? *The Westminster Shorter Catechism* provides a classic definition of Christian prayer as "an offering up of our desires unto God, for things agreeable to His will, in the name of Christ, with confession of our sins, and thankful acknowledgement of his mercies."

Imagine working for a major corporation and receiving a memo from the company's chief executive officer (CEO) inviting you to her office for an informal discussion. In the memo, you're encouraged to bring up any concern, request, or comment that is on your mind. Do you see yourself walking into the executive's grand office and, without hesitation, calling out your list of desires: more vacation, a pay raise, and greater employee benefits? Then, imagine that when you're finished, you look up at the chief and inform her that you have the utmost confidence that she is the one and only person who can fulfill all your expectations at the firm.

Such faith!

How do you think that your requests would be received by the CEO? How might such an encounter affect your relationship with the top boss? And what does it say about your future commitment to the company?

This scenario would seem absurd to most fair-minded people who take their careers seriously; yet, we as Christians frequently go before the CEO of the universe, with a similar casual attitude and self-centered motivation. For too long, we've listened to those who encourage a "name-it-and-claim-it" approach to prayer, leading us to think that if we only express sufficient belief during our "honorable" petitions, God will indeed pour out His blessings through quick affirmation—according to our expectations, of course.

Certainly, faith is that essential part of prayer which cannot be understated. Scripture tells us that faith is the very substance of all that we hope for, even when that hope has no immediate or recognizable supporting evidence (Hebrews 11:1). Paradoxically, the Bible goes on to explain that it's through faith that we gain understanding (Hebrews 11:3). How can the clarity of understanding come from a hope that lacks tangible evidence? The answer to this mystery is illustrated in the exchange that takes place between the believer and the Holy Spirit of God. So, as we step out in faith, the Spirit provides wisdom and discernment to develop a meaningful relationship with our Creator.

However, faith represents only one part in the total equation of things to consider before approaching the throne of God. In this preparation, a good place to begin is with Jesus and His example of what prayer should include:

> *Our Father which art in heaven, Hallowed be thy name. Thy kingdom come. Thy will be done in earth, as it is in heaven. Give us this day our daily bread. And forgive us our debts, as we*

forgive our debtors. And lead us not into temptation, but deliver us from evil: For thine is the kingdom, and the power, and the glory, for ever. Amen.

MATTHEW 6:9-13

Christ introduces this example by instructing his disciples to pray "after this manner". So, the inference is that a prayer may be subjective in order to reflect individual expression and needs, but constructed within a parameter, defined by God, that is honorable, loving, and worthy. In what we have long called "The Lord's Prayer," we see the divine elements of effective communication with God:

1. Addressing God—*Our Father, which art in heaven*
2. Worshiping God—*Hallowed be thy name*
3. Praying the will of God—*Thy kingdom come. Thy will be done . . .*
4. Petitioning God—*Give us this day, our daily bread*
5. Asking for forgiveness (of sins)—*forgive us of our debts*
6. Committing to forgive others—*as we forgive our debtors*
7. Humble plea for wisdom and protection—*And lead us not into temptation, but deliver us from evil*
8. Closing with praise—*For thine is the kingdom, and the power, and the glory, forever. Amen.*

A *NO* IS AS GOOD AS A *YES*

The Lord's Prayer is a thoughtful prayer, and its framework serves as a model whenever we enter into the throne room to let our requests be known to God—our Abba, Father. Nevertheless, this structure of prayer was never designed as a guarantee that all our petitions will be answered on our terms. And we often assume that our prayer has not been answered if God responds with anything other than the affirmative, *yes*. After all, is that not the answer we seek?

For example, if I ask the Lord to favor me for an existing job opportunity and He says, "No," does that mean that my prayer hasn't been answered? Of course not. The prayer has indeed been answered—and "No" was the answer.

There are other times when God may respond to our requests with, "Not now". But that answer can also be an emotional letdown, especially when our predetermined timeline is embedded within the prayer. However, the critical thing to remember on these occasions is that the Lord *always* has our best interest in mind. His concern for us becomes more apparent when we take a backward glance in our lives and see how often He has saved us from the potential disasters of our own desires. Any mature Christian will readily admit that God's greatest blessings often come through the word *no*.

If we are truly praying, "God's will be done," we should be open to whatever His answer happens to be. In fact, we should embrace every response from God with the assurance of His love and care for us.

Look again at the elements of the Lord's Prayer and note the closing remark: *For thine is the kingdom, and the power, and the glory forever. Amen.* It's a statement of praise—not dependent on God's answer. That, of course, goes against the grain of our natural desires; nevertheless, there are steps that we can take in order to experience the joy and realization of His will in our lives:

1. <u>Take the time to remember that God *always* has your best interest in mind</u>. This serves as a precursor to prayer and assures us that His response is good, just, and correct.

2. <u>Consider the framework of the Lord's Prayer and adapt it to your own prayers</u>. A redundant recitation of the Lord's Prayer—or any other prayer—is not what God seeks whenever we commune with Him. Matthew 6:7 instructs us to not use "vain repetitions". But the Lord's

Prayer can provide us with a useful template, of sorts, to help frame our thoughts and priorities as we mature in our prayer life over time.

3. <u>Transform your passions to serve God's purpose</u>. For example, everyone wants to be healthy, and when we are ill, it's common to go before God and plead, "Dear Lord, please heal my body!" We might even work ourselves into a spiritual lather and muster up the faith of a giant mustard seed in order for God to commence with His miraculous healing. After such an exercise in hyperventilated faith, how could He possibly refuse us?

Seriously though, God doesn't want His children to be sick, but as an alternative to this silly (but not uncommon) approach to prayer, first consider how you might better serve the Lord's purpose in life with a healthy body, and make that consideration your primary concern. By changing the focus of the prayer to serving God's purpose, you have neither undermined nor abandoned your petition for healing. But changing your priority and heartfelt passion will fundamentally impact both your prayer life and relationship with God.

These recommendations should also apply to requests for money, career advancement, improved human relationships, or most any desire that we would bring before the Lord. Always remember that the contentment in receiving God's answer is realized by first seeking His will. But note that prayer is not a word game or means of spiritual manipulation. God *always* knows our heart before our head is bowed. Our prayers must be sincere and coupled with the determination to follow up with the correct course of action as God directs.

This mention of spiritual manipulation reminds me of a humorous encounter that I had with my son, Gabriel, when he was just four years old. I was sitting in our living room at home and Gabe ran into the room, full of excitement.

"Dad, Dad," he said, "I want to ask you a question, and whatever I ask, you say *yes*. Okay Dad?"

"Let me see if I have this right," I replied. "You want to ask me a question, but before you do, you'd like me to say *yes* ahead of time. Is that correct?"

"Yeah, Dad, yeah!" His excitement was building with every word.

I was so charmed by that little boy and tempted to give in to his request, but I had to use this time as a teaching opportunity. I carefully explained to him that people rarely, if ever, grant our wishes by committing to a pledge that precedes our request. Life just doesn't work that way. Unfortunately, I never thought to go back and ask Gabe what his original question was. Over the decades since, I've often wondered.

This simple story sounds like something every parent might expect from their own child at that age. But did you know that Jesus experienced this same thing during His years of ministry? Now, you may think that Jesus never had any kids, but the fact is, He had twelve of them—we call them disciples. In Mark 10:35, we pick up the action:

> *Then James and John, the sons of Zebedee, came to Him, saying, "Teacher, we want You to do for us whatever we ask."*

(As though the Lord of the universe is going to fall for this line.)

> *And [Jesus] said to them, "What do you want Me to do for you?"*
> *They said to Him, "Grant us that we may sit, one on Your right hand and the other on Your left, in Your glory."*
> *But Jesus said to them, "You do not know what you ask. Are you able to drink the cup that I drink, and be baptized with the baptism that I am baptized with?"*
> *They said to Him, "We are able."*
>
> MARK 10:35-39

As Scripture points out, these two geniuses were attempting to book tickets for the best seats in the house—one on either side of Christ's throne. But Jesus patiently explained to them (and to all of us geniuses) a divine principle that true greatness is realized through sacrifice.

It's interesting to note that the disciples' request was never shattered by Jesus, rather, it was placed in the bright light of truth. This story serves as a lesson for every request that we may ever bring before God.

BE CAREFUL WHAT YOU ASK FOR

Our human nature generally desires the fruition of our human passions. But if we bother to take time and consider the outcomes of many who have pursued their passions apart from the Lord's divine guidance, we might gain a new appreciation for the restraints that God places on us.

Napoleon Bonaparte's Russian campaign presents a classic lesson in *being careful what you ask for*. As Emperor of France, Napoleon was facing the tough decision between pressing forward with his army to conquer Moscow, or postponing the campaign. With twelve years of triumphs and twenty famous victories behind him, Napoleon was in no mood to tolerate the advice of his marshals who counseled for a delayed march. To him, their caution was a sign that they were spoiled and had become weak. But the Emperor's passion to seize Russia's grand city continued to burn within his soul.

Napoleon had amassed a magnificent army, nearly a half-million strong, and in June of 1812, he led them across the Polish-Russian border near the Niemen River and into a hostile land. The events that followed will live eternal in military and European history. The French did indeed reach Moscow on September 14th and took the city, but at a tremendous cost. Bloody battles and attrition had reduced Napoleon's army down to 100,000—less than one quarter of its original size. And if that weren't bad enough, the much-needed resources of Moscow had been stripped away by a fleeing Russian army and the advancing French were left with a shell of a city.

It soon became very apparent that Napoleon's options were collapsing around him. Although the Russians had been in retreat, they still had access to resources throughout their homeland's villages and countryside. Meanwhile, the French supply lines were totally cut off and winter cold was getting ready to launch a brutal campaign of its own.

In October of that year, a desperate and disheartened French army began its dreadful retreat back home. During the journey, Napoleon abandoned his troops and left for Paris to protect his position as emperor. By the time his former grand army crossed into France that November, their numbers had been reduced to a meager 27,000 men, with over 300,000 killed and 100,000 captured.

Technically, we could argue that the campaign of Napoleon Bonaparte was a success because he had seized the city of Moscow and beat back the Russian army. But history will never record this event as a military victory for Napoleon. Instead, the campaign marked the decline of this once powerful leader.

Napoleon never sought wise counsel, and he certainly didn't seek the wisdom of God. Throughout history, there have been numerous occasions when God has allowed self-proclaimed autonomous men to pursue their own thoughts and passions. And the consequences that follow never seem to fulfill original expectations.

PRAYER AND SUFFERING

There are few petitions deemed more worthy than a prayer for physical well-being; and many times, God has responded with a "no" to such requests.

Joni Eareckson Tada is no stranger to the experience of pain and despair after calling out to God for healing. In 1967, Joni was a beautiful young lady and talented artist whose whole life was ahead of her. But in that year, she suffered a tragic diving accident while swimming, and it marked the beginning of her new life as a quadriplegic. The depth of Joni's initial despair is beyond the scope of this author to fully comprehend, but it's described with detail in her biography: *Joni Eareckson Tada's Life Story*.

My friend and pastor, Todd Rettberg, wrote his first book: *Life's a Pain: Journeying by Faith When Every Step Hurts*. In it, he shares the story of his ongoing struggle with chronic pain from daily migraine headaches. Many times, the pain is so severe that the only thing that Todd can do is lie down and suffer. And many times he has cried out to God for relief as he works to minister to the community while fulfilling his role at home as husband and dad to three active boys.

Pastor Todd, Joni Eareckson Tada, and many likeminded Christian people who suffer in life, are members of a remarkable class of folks who continually demonstrate an awareness that the rest of us (viewing from the outside) do not fully grasp. They understand that God takes hurting people, in the midst of their pain or loss, to an otherwise unattainable higher place—a place that may not be recognized or understood by the masses, but where the power and perfect will of God resides.

This has certainly been apparent in Todd's ministry; and on a larger public scale, the same is true for Joni. The work that she has done through radio, books, painting, television, and public speaking has brought healing to many others. And in the course of events, her testimony has expressed joy, with no regrets, in God's purpose for her life.

> O Lord my God, I cried unto thee, and thou has healed me.
> – Psalm 30:2 (KJV)

It's difficult to adequately address the real suffering that exists in the world. But unless we come to a point where we fully embrace a passion for living in the will of God, we'll fail to understand how our natural desires can be fulfilled through the joy and empowerment that He provides during times of need.

When our hearts and priorities are right with God, we position ourselves to receive the very best that He has for us. So often, the Lord opens doors, previously unseen, and grants us access to the very things we desire. But regardless of His response to our prayer, the fulfillment of God's grand purpose in our lives will exceed our previous hopes and greatest expectations.

BOLDNESS

> Let us therefore come boldly unto the throne of grace, that we may obtain mercy, and find grace to help in time of need.
> – Hebrews 4:16 (KJV)

Earlier, we used the analogy of a worker approaching his corporate CEO with a series of self-centered requests. In Hebrews 4:16, we see that God has given us an invitation to His "office" to present our requests to Him. Note the words "come boldly" in the Lord's invitation. What does that imply?

The offer seems to suggest that we have direct 24/7 access to God in getting our prayers answered, and we should be confident and accept this invitation with *bold* faith. But there's an element to God's proposition that's often overlooked. The fact is, *boldness* not only speaks to our faith in Him, but also to the confidence we have with our own prayer. In other words, we must take the time to examine the worthiness of our petitions by asking ourselves if they're self-centered or within God's will, in the spirit of love or the spirit of retribution, scripturally sound or carnally based—the list goes on. These are important considerations because as we bring our petitions to Him, we should be prepared to give a *bold* answer to the question: Why?

As previously stated, there's no need to disqualify our personal desires by assessing the purpose, priority, and motivation of our prayers. But in the end, approaching the Lord with *boldness* involves both faith *and* the personal confidence that our prayers are honorable, and thereby worthy, to carry into the throne room of grace and mercy.

> My words fly up, my thoughts remain below:
> Words without thoughts never to heaven go.
> — SHAKESPEARE, *HAMLET*

CHAPTER SIX

The Good Ol' Days

A signed limited edition of G. Harvey's *Charity, The Gift of Love*, hangs in our living room. It's an image that depicts an early twentieth-century street scene with glistening rain-soaked sidewalks and glowing lamps in nearby windows. Twilight hangs over the city. A horse and carriage are parked at the curb and a little girl stands in the walkway with her mother, offering a bouquet of flowers to an elderly woman seated on a bench. Gazing into this peaceful scene, I begin to hear the soft murmur of voices as pedestrians, dressed in their stylish hats and long coats, converse with one another, and the sound of an old Model-T working its way up the cobblestone street. It's an instance of time and place where all is well in the world.

> Life can only be understood backwards; but it must be lived forwards.
> – SOREN KIERKEGAARD, *1813-1855*

What a contrast this picture provides when compared to twenty-first century urban life. Beyond the hustle and bustle of modern cities, there's the reported escalation of crime, corruption, and bankruptcy. Detroit serves as a heartbreak tale of a once proud metropolis and king of the industrial age—a town that produced the greatest automobiles in the world. At its peak, Detroit was home to 1.9 million residents, but it never recovered from the riots of 1967, and today it's a broken city of about 600,000 with no way to meet its financial obligations. Many watch this city as though it were a canary in a mineshaft; a harbinger of things to come in America. Detroit isn't the only urban casualty in modern times. Chicago has gained a national reputation as a city of rapidly surging crime and fiscal mismanagement. Even smaller towns, such as San Bernardino, California face bankruptcy, while a growing number of municipalities struggle to sustain vibrant business communities, improve conditions in the overcrowded schools, and reign in extravagant public expenditures.

Despite these problems, America continues to be a blessed nation, although it currently stands at the crossroads of economic uncertainty and global unrest. Regardless of the political persuasion of its citizens, many are wondering what the future of America will look like. Even the United States Constitution is increasingly being criticized by some as an outdated document, unable to meet the needs of a twenty-first century society.

Perhaps the generation that holds the fondest memories of America is that of the baby-boomers (so called for their booming birthrate from 1946 to 1964). This is especially true for the earlier boomers who, on balance, lived in the best of times. Of course, things weren't perfect by any means. Events during the civil rights movement in the early sixties serve as a vivid reminder that the country had not yet brought closure to the existing strife in race relations. And the threat of a nuclear attack from the Soviet Union caused many homeowners to consider installing residential bomb shelters, while their kids participated in duck-and-cover drills as a normal part of school life.

Nevertheless, America was largely beaming with optimism and a boundless hope for the future. The country had recently won its second world war with the unconditional surrender from both Germany and Japan—and the cost of that war was paid for by the generation that fought it. These were the parents, aunts and uncles of the baby-boomers and referred to by demographers as the *silent generation*. They paved the way for an immense period of economic expansion and technological advancement. This was the world that the boomers were born into, and they received the harvest of all that had been previously sown through blood and sacrifice.

Television itself was a baby-boomer in its own right. Never mind the fact that early programing was bland and corny—that was part of its charm. Besides, at the time no one knew any better. The fact that families could have a window to the world in their own living rooms was amazing, and the technology just kept getting better. In 1954, NBC broadcasted the first coast-to-coast color program, showing the Rose Parade to the 200 sets capable of receiving its color signal. The major networks of that time were the *only* networks: ABC, NBC and CBS[5]. Before long, their lineup of memorable programs, ranging from "The Ed Sullivan Show" to "Bonanza" to "Perry Mason" to "I Love Lucy," created a new experience in American entertainment. And who among early baby-boomers can forget the age of *Route 66* and those marvelous *See the USA in your Chevrolet* jingles?

Although the years from the 1950s to early '60s were not without problems, the period represents a season wherein fond memories of a simpler, yet more vibrant America are easy to extrapolate. As the country began to modernize, there were real heroes and a real sense of adventure for young people. It was a season that baby-boomers thought would never end.

> Deep as love,
> Deep as first love, and wild with all regret;
> O Death in Life, the days that are no more!
> — Alfred, Lord Tennyson, *The Princess*.

---

[5] DuMont Television Network sought to establish a competitive position among ABC, CBS and NBC, but didn't succeed financially. It ceased operations in 1956.

There's a common word used to capture this fond backward glance in time; we call it *nostalgia*. By definition, nostalgia is "a wistful sentimental yearning for something past or irrecoverable." This sentiment is so strong that an entire industry has been built around it: antique shops, old movies, period art works, classic pop music, and of course, those beautiful automobiles. Collectively, this market genre accounts for millions of dollars in trade, largely due to the demographic of baby-boomers who rely on it to help preserve a way of life that is vanishing before their eyes.

But does the Bible have anything to say about the sentiment of nostalgia? In fact, it does. Scripture takes both a strong and paradoxical position on this subject. Although the Old and New Testaments largely speak to us from a historical perspective, they clearly reveal God's unfavorable view of man's tendency to live in the past.

King Solomon writes,

> "Do not say, 'Why were the former days better than these?' For you do not inquire wisely concerning this."
>
> ECCLESIASTES 7:10 (NKJV)

By the same token, the prophet Isaiah tells the Israelites to not live for "the former things" in life because God will do new things and "make a way in the wilderness" (Isaiah 43:18-19).

In addition to simply having fond memories of past events, nostalgia is often embraced when the present time period becomes difficult or unfamiliar. The Hebrew children of the Exodus serve as a perfect example. After four hundred years of slavery, they were ready to return to Egypt because the familiarity of enslavement (with "three hots and a cot") seemed the better option when compared to the daily menu served on the road to the Promised Land.

We know that nothing much has changed with mankind over the years. The real truth behind nostalgia is that it rarely considers all the facts of past events. Nostalgia is primarily fueled by our selective memories and resides as a subjective ideal in our hearts and minds. In reality, we only take from the past what we desire.

In late 1989, the Berlin Wall (along with the image of the *Iron Curtain*) was torn down and it marked the end of an era for the soviet empire. The event was broadcast over television and the free world shared in the greatest celebration since WWII. However, it wasn't long after this historical jubilee that reality set in. Within two or three years, east Berliners discovered that liberty and the free market system demanded self-discipline, new methodologies, and a new way of thinking. As a result, many began to call for a return to the familiarity of communism, even though it represented a life of oppression for over seventy years.

In Budapest, Hungary (of all places), a popular café called the Marxim Restaurant celebrates the days of Lenin and Stalin with its Communist "Party" atmosphere and barbed wire décor—never mind the fact that Budapest was bombed by soviet planes, and still displays many pockmark scars from soviet tanks firing on city buildings during the invasion of 1956. But the Marxim doesn't focus on this part of history. Instead, as one patron reports on the Internet: the restaurant "is really cool" along with good food and "funny stuff pertaining to the communist years."

BAD MEMORIES

Although nostalgia is widely manifested in various forms, there are people who possess few fond memories from their past. Rather than extrapolating images of good times, an individual may recall only hurt, regret, and pain. After every effort is made to avoid painful thoughts of yesteryear, memories may still refuse to turn loose of one's mind and spirit. Over time, that individual may be robbed of the necessary strength and desire to advance into the future with confidence.

Several years ago, I caught a last minute flight from southern California to Charlotte, North Carolina to attend the memorial service for my deceased brother-in-law. During the final leg of my trip, I pulled out a business magazine that I had purchased during a layover. An article featuring advice from some of the leading business giants in industry caught my eye—especially one story in particular. During this interview, the author asked the CEO of a major global firm to share any insight gained through his years of experience. The executive told the story of a time when he and his family were vacationing in India where they had an opportunity to travel on a guided safari, riding large pachyderms across the landscape. At predetermined points of interest along the route, the group would stop and dismount as their guide prepared to secure each elephant. He began by driving a steel stake about one foot deep into the ground with a small but weighty hammer, and repeated this task in front of each animal. Next, he walked down the line and took the leader rope of each elephant and quickly hitched it around the driven stake in front of them.

The executive became intrigued as he observed the guide's method of securing each of these majestic beasts. He asked the guide what kept an elephant from simply raising its head and pulling the stake out of the ground and setting itself free. Surely, a small stake—only one foot deep—couldn't adequately hold such a large animal in place against its own will.

"You are right," replied the guide, "The elephant can easily lift up his head and pull the stake out of the ground. But he doesn't know that."

The guide went on to explain that when an elephant is a baby, he's tied under the same conditions. The baby will pull several times against the stake, but cannot set himself free. From that time forward, the baby will grow into an adult with the belief that he cannot pull the stake out of the ground. At that moment, the executive thought of all the people he had known in business who demonstrated the same affliction as those elephants—people who were capable of much greater things in life, but were somehow tied to the stake of their own memories and imaginations, unable to lift their heads and set themselves free.

> But thou, O Lord, art a shield about me; my glory, and the One who lifts my head.
> – PSALM 3:3

It's essential to understand that the Bible places a value on the past inasmuch as its history establishes a divine principle, or serves to remind us of an event with eternal significance. In other words, the past serves to prepare us for the future. It's not designed by God to give us a place to "live" through our collected memories—good or bad. This has been true from the very beginning when the Lord set a rainbow in the sky as a reminder of how He delivered Noah and his family from the catastrophic flood of earth (Genesis 9:16). That same rainbow also served as a promise for the future, declaring that the Lord will never again destroy the world by flood.

Biblical examples of God pointing to the past for reflection of His glory and love towards mankind are almost too many to list. Nevertheless, it's our duty as believers to seek out these lessons in Scripture and apply them to our lives as we continually move forward in time. Our tradition of Holy Communion provides us with the opportunity for our greatest reflection of the past. The bread and cup remind us of the foundational truth of the Christian faith through the broken body and shed blood of Jesus Christ. The significance of His ancient sacrifice on the cross encompasses each day of endless tomorrows.

Remember too that the ceremonies and traditions of Christ followers need not be restricted to a procedure outlined from the biblical record. As Christians, we have the freedom to celebrate any honorable event with proper focus and the spirit of truth. For example, every Thanksgiving and Christmas holiday serves as a blessed time of enormous gratitude, reflection, and worship for what God has done on our behalf.

WHAT'S IN A WORD?

In conclusion, it's worth noting the origin of the word, *nostalgia*. It comes from the Greek word, *nostos*, and means "coming home". So, the question before us is: *Where is our home?* As Christians, it's more than a habitat; it's an appointed destination that resides in our future, and not in our past. In fact, it is the kingdom of Heaven. Therefore, in the spirit of true *nostos*, let us not live in "the days that are no more," but continually look ahead with confidence, towards the high calling of God through Christ Jesus.

CHAPTER SEVEN

The Power Behind Humility

Of all the virtues in Christian doctrine, nothing has eluded me more than a true understanding of humility. In one sense, I could comprehend how a person's humble spirit could reflect the image of Christ, but maintaining such an obsequious demeanor in a dog-eat-dog world was quite another story. Without an injection of backbone and fortitude, a person would likely be subjugated to a permanent underclass. From my observations, respect always followed after strength, and I saw no value in sheepishly hanging my head down before people who would be happy to exploit me at every opportunity. What glory or testimony could ever come from that?

On the other hand, I never felt compelled to participate in altercations involving mindless quarrels over senseless issues. It was better for me to walk away from such encounters, even if it appeared to be a sign of weakness. Someone once said, "Never argue with a moron, because he'll drag you down to his level and beat you with experience." The statement may seem a bit crude, but there's a significant truth behind it.

> And a servant of the Lord must not quarrel but be gentle to all, able to teach, patient, in humility correcting those who are in opposition, if God perhaps will grant them repentance, so that they may know the truth, and that they may come to their senses and escape the snare of the devil, having been taken captive by him to do his will.
> – II Timothy 2:24-26 (NKJV)

Despite its virtue, the divine calling to live a humble life would seem to conflict with the idea of not casting one's pearls before swine (Matthew 7:6), because the pigs will only trample them and turn again to devour you.

In the natural sense, humility appears to be counterproductive in a world that often demands assertiveness. In such an environment, the humble believer is like a puzzle piece that doesn't fit into the broader picture. After all, wouldn't a successful Christian witness be demonstrated through confidence, purpose, and authority? How then, would humility serve this end?

In His sermon on the mount, Jesus stated:

> *Blessed are the meek, for they shall inherit the earth.*
> Matthew 5:5, (NKJV)

Taken at face value, this scripture seems to fail at conforming to the visible realities of this world. If the *meek* do not contend for place and position, how do they expect to "inherit the earth"—or anything else for that matter? It appears that the reward for the humble won't be realized until the far distant future. In the meantime, the abject believer is supposed to willingly place himself in a state of ongoing privation. In so doing, he becomes a lagging entity in a hazardous world that is changing with increasing velocity.

During the early years of my Christian life, these impressions framed my intellectual and emotional struggle with every notion of living a humble life. I simply couldn't resolve my conflict with being in God's perfect will through timidity, vulnerability, weakness, and ineffectiveness.

I had a lot to learn about the subject of humility.

THE "PERFECT" MAN

Ask anyone familiar with the Old Testament book of Job to give you a one-sentence description of his story, and they may respond with something like: "Job was a man of God, made whole after his faith withstood many trials." And that pretty much described my assessment after reading Job, hearing the sermons, and discussing his epic story in numerous Bible studies. In its essence, the book of Job was all about how God restores the faithful—or so I thought.

For more than a decade, I have repeatedly enjoyed reading the Bible through, from cover to cover. One summer evening, I was alone in our family reading room and, once again, incrementally working my way from Genesis through Revelation. On this occasion, I was in the book of Job; naturally projecting how his tribulation would end since I already knew the story from start to finish. The scripture wasted no time in declaring that Job was blameless, upright, and a man who feared God and despised evil (Job 1:1). In fact, God *Himself* told Satan that there was no man on earth whose righteousness compared to that of Job (v.8). By any human measure, Job was the perfect man.

But this story left open questions in my mind that had not been fully resolved. What motivated God to accept Satan's conniving challenge to test Job's faith through such a painful experiment? And what is the significant lesson that all future generations need to take away from this story?

> You have become cruel to me; with the strength of Your hand You oppose me. You lift me up to the wind and cause me to ride on it; You spoil my success.
>
> – Job 30:21-22 (NKJV)

Anyone familiar with Job's plight knows that he suffered in ways that most of us cannot imagine. God only restricted Satan's antagonistic powers by not allowing him to kill His servant during this affliction. Consequently, Job's loss was all-inclusive, except for life itself. Crime, death, destruction, and disease were all around him. And his bewilderment over God's sudden and aggressive action—seemingly punitive in nature—added to his suffering.

Initial advice came from Job's wife who recommended that he "curse God and die." Then, his three friends, Eliphaz, Bildad, and Zophar, came to comfort him, but ended up callously accusing him of pride and hypocrisy before the Lord. The full brunt of Job's new reality left him with an overwhelming sense of hopelessness and despair:

> *"May the day perish on which I was born,*
> *And the night in which it was said,*
> *'A male child is conceived.'*
> *May that day be darkness;*
> *May God above not seek it,*
> *Nor the light shine upon it.*
> *May darkness and the shadow of death claim it;*
> *May a cloud settle on it;*
> *May the blackness of the day terrify it.*
> *As for that night, may darkness seize it;*
> *May it not rejoice among the days of the year,*
> *May it not come into the number of the months.*

> *Oh, may that night be barren!*
> *May no joyful shout come into it!*
> *May those curse it who curse the day,*
> *Those who are ready to arouse Leviathan.*
> *May the stars of its morning be dark;*
> *May it look for light, but have none,*
> *And not see the dawning of the day;*
> *Because it did not shut up the doors of my mother's womb,*
> *Nor hide sorrow from my eyes.*
> *Why did I not die at birth?*
> *Why did I not perish when I came from the womb?*
>
> Job 3:3-11 (KJV)

Next, Job does something that any believer in God would do: he attempts to rationalize his present situation. He is now conflicted over the purpose behind these afflictions and strives to identify a sin in his life that may have gone unnoticed. If any shortcoming is found, he will immediately seek forgiveness; but nothing comes to mind. Again, Job calls out to God for an answer, but there is no answer. In the meantime, his friends continue their poetic assaults on his spiritual character.

At the time, I was failing to fully comprehend this story. The takeaway from my assessment of Job's plight was simply aligned with the popular notion that God restores the faithful; and eventually, Job was indeed restored. But though I had accepted this premise as truth, something seemed to be missing within it—a backstory, an unresolved mystery, but one that I could never quite define. After all, the idea of God as the restorer is continually reinforced in Scripture. Why then, would Job need to endure such extreme suffering in order to confirm something so obviously demonstrated throughout the biblical record? Was there anything else to consider that would make the essence of this story something more than a redundant theme of deliverance?

By chapter 38, all the words and platitudes of Job and his friends have been spoken; and now, the Lord has arrived on the scene. His entrance out of the whirlwind provides an image of the omnipotent schoolmaster who is about to deliver a pop-quiz to His students. And the students are not prepared.

God wastes no time in getting to the point:

> *"Who is this who darkens counsel by words without knowledge? Now prepare yourself like a man; I will question you, and you shall answer Me.*
>
> *"Where were you when I laid the foundations of the earth? Tell Me, if you have understanding."*
>
> Job 38:2-4 (NKJV)

At first glance, it's hard to understand how a loving God could be so insensitive to Job's sufferings. The Lord's engaging entrance seemed more personal to me when I considered the fact that I wouldn't fair as well as Job under similar circumstances. But as I continued to read these passages in the solitude of God's spirit, He revealed to me the deeper meaning that had escaped me for so many years.

Indeed, there was another element to Job's story that put everything into perspective; and the mystery was revealed by Job *himself*. It was in chapter 42 where Job, awestruck and exhausted, finally responded to the words of God. After verses 5 and 6, my reading stopped cold:

> *"I have heard of You by the hearing of the ear, but now my eye sees You. Therefore I abhor myself, and repent in dust and ashes."*

The mystery behind the book's essential meaning is revealed in the question: Why would a perfect man abhor himself?

During his excellent work in the video series, *The Truth Project* (a production of *Focus On the Family*), Dr. Del Tackett states, "When we behold the face of God, it exposes us for who we really are."[6] That is exactly what happened to Job in chapter 42. Not only did he see God, he simultaneously saw himself—for the first time! But no longer was he the "perfect man". Rather, he was a man diminished before an almighty God, but a God who ultimately restored and empowered his servant beyond measure. And in the end, the future for Eliphaz, Bildad, and Zophar was dependent on both their obedience to God *and* Job's personal recommendation regarding them.

Humility is a large part of the essential lesson of Job for all future generations. We simply cannot be good enough (i.e., *perfect*) through our own strength, and we must never fail to seek the virtues that can only be found through a humble life. This is where real power begins for the believer.

THE PROPHET

Job's self-exposure before the face of God is not unique in Scripture. In Isaiah, chapter 6, we see that the prophet had a vision in which he "saw the Lord sitting on a throne, high and lifted up". Isaiah's reaction to this vision was very similar to Job's when he proclaimed in verse 5:

> *Woe is me, for I am undone!*
> *Because I am a man of unclean lips,*
> *And I dwell in the midst of a people of unclean lips;*
> *For my eyes have seen the King, the Lord of hosts.*

Two things, previously mentioned, are present here: First of all, Isaiah is exposed as he sees God "sitting on a throne," and is thereby humbled. Secondly, Isaiah's epiphany not only unmasks his own weaknesses, but simultaneously reveals to him the weaknesses of *all* humanity. He instantly

---

6   The Truth Project, Lesson 1: Veritology – What is Truth?

realizes that he lives among people much like himself—that is, people with unclean lips. Once again, this second point serves to confirm that true humility *does not* involve personal inferiority. Rather, it empowers Isaiah and makes way for clear thinking as it prepares the prophet for the high calling that God has placed on his life.

THE PERFECT MARRIAGE

There are two types of discipline in life: The first application refers to the discipline that is imposed on us from a higher authority; the second reflects the discipline that we impose on ourselves. In the halls of learning, it's hoped that the external source of discipline primes the student for a lifestyle of self-discipline where joy and the satisfaction of meaningful accomplishment reside.

Voluntary submission is an observable work of self-discipline; but like humility, it suffers from a growing disdain in modern Western culture. It's not that the idea of submission is necessarily offensive, as long as someone else is doing the submitting. Both men and women often resent the idea of consenting to another person's authority or position—especially if they don't respect that individual. Even tacit acquiescence goes against our grain. It's as though our hearts were branded at birth with the message: *My way or the highway!*

The Bible has a lot to say about submission. Examples include submitting to one another in the fear of Christ (Ephesians 5:21), servants submit to masters (I Peter 2:18), young people submit to elders (I Peter 5:5), just to mention a few. But when it comes to implementing the principle of submission in our most important social relationship, nothing compares to marriage.

> Wives, submit yourselves unto your own husbands, as unto the Lord. For the husband is the head of the wife, even as Christ is the head of the church: and he is the Savior of the body. Therefore as the church is subject unto Christ, so let the wives be to their own husbands in every thing. Husbands, love your wives, even as Christ also loved the church, and gave himself for it.
>
> – Ephesians 5:22 (KJV)

It's the institution of marriage that sets the foundation for society. When the family unit isn't healthy, society suffers. But even though the bond between husband and wife is so crucial, the migration towards new social norms is making marital submission wildly unpopular—and this also applies to marriages within the body of Christ.

There's a reason for this unpopularity. It goes back to the topic of God's paradigm in the chapter *The God Who Is*. Because of sin, we fail to see things the way God does. As a result, our acts of rebellion are almost always built on wrong premises.

It's often been said that *money makes the world go 'round.* In Western culture—certainly, in America—those who possess the greatest wealth and position typically have the greatest authority. In recent decades, women have emerged with a formidable presence in this new world of opportunity. No longer is the production of wealth largely dependent on sweat and muscle, as in the past. Wealth creation in the twenty-first century is fundamentally tied directly to knowledge. It's the age of information, and in this environment, women bring plenty to the table. Despite recent downturns in the economy, women have gained prominent positions in industry, government, education, science, and nearly every institution in existence. The

American woman now realizes that the ranks of authority in both public and private institutions are within her reach. And regardless of the ongoing public discourse over equal opportunity, it's undeniable that women have become much more empowered than ever before. This advancement will no doubt continue as long as the mantra for wealth creation remains: *Knowledge is power!*

Although the gender wage gap shows that men are still out-earning women, the gap has steadily narrowed by more than 14 percent since 1951. This trend leads the popular media to project an image of womanhood with a greater sense of independence and autonomy. These dynamics work together to create a *new norm* in how husbands and wives relate to one another—and the Biblical standard of submission is not a part of that norm.

In order to gain an understanding of the true intent of marital submission (or any application of submission), it's essential that all Scripture on this subject be considered, and not just the *wives, submit to husbands* part.

What's being described in these verses is the perfect marriage relationship, superimposed on the image of Christ and His church. It is perfect because it's designed by God. In this design, the wife submits to the headship of her husband. Her submission empowers the husband; but he doesn't leverage that empowerment for his own self-interest. Instead, he uses it to serve the interest of his wife, and puts her and the family ahead of himself.

As this model is perfected over time, the family unit becomes a self-nurturing closed system—a well-oiled machine. Submission within this complex is a bilateral activity, an ongoing cooperative action, and expressed through the independent role of each spouse. In this mutually beneficial love relationship, all needs are met. From the honeymoon to the parting death, submission has absolutely *nothing* to do with power and control; but, it has *everything* to do with synergy.

THE PERFECT SON

Jesus' parable of the prodigal son, in Luke chapter 15, is really a tale about *two* sons. It's an allegory with universal significance because the story represents the love of God (expressed in the character of the father), towards humanity (both sons, with very human traits). This is one of the better-known stories in the Bible, and although it illustrates a truth for both men and women, the storyline really connects with any man who has ever attempted to sow his wild oats at an early age.

As is often the case, these two siblings are polar opposites. The older son has been dutifully working within his father's estate and following instructions. He's played by the rules all his life. Then one day, he sees his younger brother do something unimaginable by going to their father and requesting the immediate withdrawal of his inheritance. With sadness, the father capitulates.

It's interesting to note that the younger son felt compelled to journey "to a far country" after receiving his newfound wealth. The act of rebelling against one's parent instinctively calls for a lot of separation, and the boy wanted to put as much real estate between himself and his father as possible. This faraway land would allow the youngster to maximize both his sovereignty *and* stupidity. After a famine arose in the land, the son's resources were depleted and it didn't take long for him to see the reality of his situation. The party was over and desperation was now on the horizon. In despair, the son took an entry level position, feeding the swine of a local farmer; it soon became apparent that these pigs were going to be the boy's new peer group.

There are times in life when a man can't see *up* until he can no longer go further downward. It was at this point where the son "came to himself" and realized that his father's servants were treated better and were well fed. This moment was pivotal for the young son, and he humbly returned to the father, confessed his sin, and asked for mercy and forgiveness.

During this father-son reunion, the older brother was working in the fields. When he returned to the house, there was the sound of music, dancing, and the aroma of good food on the grill. He then beheld his younger sibling, standing there in his father's finest robe and sandals, with a big ring on his finger. This kid was the center of attention at his father's grand celebration!

The scene immediately provoked the older son to such anger that he refused to take part in the despicable event. After obeying the rules and working hard, he felt insulted by this display of attention toward his contemptuous brother. But his father came out and pleaded with his older son and expressed his love for both him and his younger sibling.

> "And he said to him, 'Son, you are always with me, and all that I have is yours. It was right that we should make merry and be glad, for your brother was dead and is alive again, and was lost and is found.'"
>
> – Luke 15:31-32 (NKJV)

The story of the prodigal son gives us an excellent view from within the paradigm of God; first, by contrasting two very real characteristics of human nature, and then demonstrating His love through the celebration of a changed life. And although the obedience of the older son represents an essential part of a relationship with the Father, it does not complete that relationship. Obedience must include humility, repentance and compassion. It's at that point that we learn what love is really all about.

THE IMPERFECT MAN

The apostle Paul provides yet another example of the power behind humility. The apostle was anything but perfect during his life. Scripture introduces Paul in Acts chapter 7, in his former identity as Saul of Tarsus; a man of authority with the blood of saints on his hands. But though Saul was not walking with God, as Job had, he nevertheless sought to do God's will—in his own mind—by persecuting an upstart Christian movement in order to keep the law and established doctrine pure from what he believed to be heresy.

> As he journeyed he came near Damascus, and suddenly a light shone around him from heaven. Then he fell to the ground, and heard a voice saying to him, "Saul, Saul, why are you persecuting Me?" And he said, "Who are You, Lord?" Then the Lord said, "I am Jesus, whom you are persecuting..."
> – Acts 9:3-5 (NKJV)

During a business trip, of sorts, to conduct further tyranny in Damascus, Saul beheld the face of God and was temporarily blinded by His presence. The encounter not only exposed Saul for his true self, it denuded everything he believed to be true up to that moment. In time, Saul of Tarsus became known as Paul, a follower of Christ, and totally committed to the gospel of salvation. But it took a while for believers to overcome their fear of Paul and the memories they carried of him.

No doubt, the stigma of having persecuted innocent believers—people he now loved—weighed heavily on the apostle's conscience. Throughout his remarkable missionary journey, Paul repeatedly proclaimed that he was the *least* of all the saints. But humility and repentance had empowered Paul, giving him a greater determination to do the will of God, preach the gospel, start the church movement, and change the world.

> The reward of humility and the fear of the Lord are riches, honor and life.
> – Proverbs 22:4 (NASB)

Humility is not the supposed weakness of character as commonly perceived through a distorted world view. Instead, humility prepares us for clarity of thought by replacing deceptive pride (and its associated arrogance) with a focus on reality; clearing our minds for objective thinking. With all the important decisions that life demands of us, rational thought and wisdom become priceless gifts from God, and they can only mature through a submissive heart and humble spirit.

CHAPTER EIGHT

Fear

In the dark waters of the North Atlantic, about four hundred nautical miles south of Newfoundland, a fearful message was delivered to the bridge of the RMS Titanic. Up to that moment, the pride of the British builders, White Star Line, had completed most of its maiden voyage from Southampton, UK to New York City, providing world class luxury for its privileged elite passengers. Second and third class travelers, many seeking a better life, were also a part of this celebrated historic passage. But on April 14, 1912 at 11:40 p.m. (ship's time), a crisis was unfolding.

Great Brittan's Olympic-class ocean liner was on a collision course with a medium-sized iceberg and First Officer William Murdoch ordered immediate evasive maneuvers. "Hard-a-starboard!" he called over to the bridge, hoping to steer the Titanic around the frozen mass.[7] As an added measure, Murdoch reportedly ordered the engines reversed, hoping to avoid, or at least minimize impact. But the reverse thrust only slowed the Titanic's ability

---

7 Louise Patten, granddaughter of Titanic's Second Officer, Charles Lightoller, claimed that the command "Hard-a-starboard" was misinterpreted by the helmsman who applied the British tiller navigation method, steering the ship in an unintended direction. This action would have turned the Titanic into the iceberg rather than away from it—opposite to Murdoch's command.

to complete its turn and the mighty 46,000 ton ship ran its starboard side along the iceberg, ripping a hole over 200 feet long into its hull plating. The resulting inflow of sea water soon flooded forward compartments, taking the ship's front half below the surface. With its bow angled downward, the huge ocean liner broke in two, and within three hours, the majestic "unsinkable ship" slipped under the frigid waters of the Atlantic. The tragic loss of life continued for a short while until more than 1,500 passengers and crew members perished at sea.

This historic event has captured the imagination of many and created a mountain of research over the years. Forensic discoveries continue even today, and a number of experts believe that the Titanic would likely have survived the event if First Officer Murdoch had elected to strike the threatening iceberg head-on, rather than expose the ship's vulnerable starboard side to the impact. Of course, we may never know for sure as explorers and researchers continue to debate the details of the Titanic's demise. But this tragic incident provides us with an important lesson in how we all share the capacity for putting forth our best human efforts in an attempt to avoid danger, only to make matters worse in the end.

THE FEAR FACTOR

Since we are created in the image of God, we possess an orientation towards the preservation of life. Fear effectively serves that instinct when it acts as an alert for us to initiate a corrective action when the need arises. However, fear can also become our worst enemy when it seizes our imagination and either renders us helpless, or causes us to overreact. The manifestation of this most insufferable of human emotions has been the subject of endless study and debate. But because this book seeks to delve into the paradigm of God, we, as believers, must consider how our fears play into *His* perspective and perfect will for our lives.

To begin, it's important to note that our common assumptions about fear generally depend on the different applications and extremes of its dreadful occurrences. A sudden fright is not the same experience as a foreboding thought or paranoia, but both could be classified as a type of fear.

On the other hand, fear can refer to an expressed reverence that one has for another individual, entity, or institution. But regardless of its context, fear is an intrinsic part of the human experience; it affects our development in both the physical and spiritual realms.

It's good to know that something which occupies such an elevated position among our basic human concerns is well covered in both the Old and New Testaments. But rather than attempt to tackle all the ramifications of fear, we'll take a high-level look at what the Bible tells us about this word, how it's applied, and how we should respond.

> And we have known and believed the love that God has for us. God is love, and he who abides in love abides in God, and God in him. Love has been perfected among us in this: that we may have boldness the day of judgment; because as He is, so are we in this world. There is no fear in love; but perfect love casts out fear, because fear involves torment. But he who fears has not been made perfect in love.
> – I JOHN 4:16-18 (NKJV)

It's interesting to see how God's word establishes a correlation between two seemingly unrelated concepts. The apostle John's unconventional declaration in verse 18, *"There is no fear in love; but perfect love casts out fear . . ."* might leave most of us scratching our heads. The idea of overcoming fear with something as basic as love goes against the grain of natural thought. But then again, Scripture is presenting the truth through God's perspective and we are summoned to pursue its deeper meaning.

John's reference to *the love* that "casts out fear" actually speaks to the power of God's perfect love (*agapé*) over the many dreaded fears (*phobos*) of human life. This strange fission between love and fear seems counterintuitive to our natural way of thinking, but it's one of the many mysteries that are revealed to us as we enter into the paradigm of God through the renewing of our minds. Such a transition is essential to a maturing faith. Through divine spiritual understanding, we discover that perfect love is much more than just a sentiment or ideal. The supernatural love of God displaces fear with a growing affection for both Christ *and* humanity, coupled with a contempt for sin and everything it represents. Increasing love creates a greater awareness of the contrast between good and evil, righteousness and unrighteousness, obedience and disobedience. In time, this discernment begins to realign our passions and priorities according to the Holy Spirit. As a result, fear loses its foothold on the things we were previously compelled to protect at all cost—even life itself.

GODLY FEAR

As previously mentioned, fear may refer to a reverence that one has for another. The Hebrew word, *yare*,[8] is commonly used in the Old Testament to describe fear in this context. However, the expression also includes an emotional sense of awe. It is this obeisant fear that man must have towards God—a commission that is repeated throughout the Bible. One such pronouncement is made by Solomon in the book of Ecclesiastes:

> *Let us hear the conclusion of the whole matter:*
>
> *Fear God and keep His commandments, for this is man's all. For God will bring every work into judgment including every secret thing, whether good or evil.*
>
> Ecclesiastes 12:13-14 (NKJV)

---

8   Other OT verses use the word *yirah*, carrying the similar message of reverence as *yare*.

The fear of God encompasses everything that we hope to be *in* Him and *through* Him. In such a committed relationship, we become empowered when our primary focus is on a love for God, followed by a love for our fellow man— the two greatest commandments given to us by Christ. Moreover, a real fear (*yare*) of God works to overcome (and overwhelm) carnal fears as our primary concern to please Him through faith and obedience increases over time.

> And Jesus answered him, The first of all the commandments is, Hear, O Israel; The Lord our God is one Lord: And thou shalt love the Lord thy God with all thy heart, and with all thy soul, and with all thy mind, and with all thy strength: this is the first commandment. And the second is like, namely this, Thou shalt love thy neighbor as thyself. There is none other commandment greater than these.
> – Mark 12:29-31 (KJV)

CONNECTING THE DOTS

Like so many elements within God's instructions for life, the victory over *phobos* fear is interconnected to other concepts. We can readily understand how trials and hope work together, or how discipline and maturity relate, but now we see that there is this unorthodox connection between love (*agapè*) and fear. Beyond our statement of faith, a genuine love for God compels us towards a reverent fear of Him. And yet, that same love "casts out" other fears that arise from the threatening things that may come our way in life. This can only occur as God empowers us, through His Spirit, with the understanding that life's hazards are not only temporary, but during their lifecycles, remain under the authority of His management.

God's call on the life of Jeremiah provides us with further insight on fear and, upon examination, raises an interesting question which will be mentioned later. In the opening verses of Jeremiah chapter 1, the Lord's first words to this young man who will become a prophet are both comprehensive and profound:

> *Now the word of the Lord came to me saying,*
> *"Before I formed you in the womb I knew you,*
> *And before you were born I consecrated you;*
> *I have appointed you a prophet to the nations."*
>
> Jeremiah 1: 4-5 (NASB)

In this opening statement, God has announced to Jeremiah:

1. I made you.
2. I knew you before you were born.
3. I have set you aside from all others.
4. I have appointed you.

Jeremiah has just received the declaration of his Creator's omnipotent power and authority. It's important to understand the significance of this message in order to appreciate the command that follows in verse 8:

> *"Do not be afraid of them,*
> *For I am with you to deliver you," declares the Lord."*

The words "afraid of *them*" in verse 8 refer to the wicked—those who have forsaken God, and who will hate Jeremiah. But it's the Lord's warning in verse 17 that raises a new question:

> *"Now, gird up your loins and arise, and speak to them all which I command you. Do not be dismayed before them, or I will dismay you before them."*

Note the second sentence of verse 17. God has commanded Jeremiah to *not fear them* by being dismayed, or he will suffer the consequences and look foolish (or worse) before his detractors. Now, the question arises: Is *fear* a sin?

In the common sense, we don't equate human fear as a sin against God for several reasons. First, fear doesn't fit the template of Satan's workflow that was addressed in *The Perpetual Force*, the chapter on sin. After all, who would ever lust after fear?

Secondly, we tend to see a fear-stricken individual as the victim, not the transgressor. People don't willfully subject themselves to fear. It's more natural to dodge a threat and avoid its consequences if possible. But when avoidance to a perceived danger constitutes disobedience to God, it becomes a matter of faith, and this speaks to our perception of God's omnipotence and care over us.

As we take another look at God's word to Jeremiah in chapter 1, verses 4 and 5, we see that the Lord has made Himself known and established the authority of His instruction. And the directive to "not be afraid" (v.8) is an essential part of that instruction. Again, we see the warning of verse 17 if Jeremiah disobeys and becomes "dismayed" before men.

At this point, we should note the context of the potential fear that presents itself to Jeremiah. It's not like the fear of being trapped in a burning house; however, it's more than merely an intimidation from speaking God's word to the wicked in Israel and Judah. Jeremiah will soon understand that he will be ostracized, beaten, imprisoned, and possibly killed. Under these conditions, who wouldn't be afraid?

> But I was like a gentle lamb led to the slaughter;
> And I did not know that they had devised plots against me, saying,
> "Let us destroy the tree with its fruit,
> And let us cut him off from the land of the living,
> That his name be remembered no more."
> — JEREMIAH 11: 19 (NASB)

On the surface of this encounter between God and Jeremiah, it would appear that the Lord has placed His servant in an unfair situation that is destined for catastrophic failure. But in order to fully comprehend this appointment, we must seek God's wisdom and identify the elements at work here.

> "Do not be afraid of them, for I am with you to deliver you," declares the Lord. Then the Lord stretched out His hand and touched my mouth, and the Lord said to me, "Behold, I have put My words in your mouth. See, I have appointed you this day over the nations and over the kingdoms, to pluck up and to break down, to destroy and to overthrow, to build and to plant."
> – JEREMIAH 1:8-10 (NASB)

God has not left Jeremiah high and dry; He has empowered the prophet with both the words to speak and the authority over nations. Most importantly, God has placed a calling on Jeremiah's life that will serve a much greater purpose than he can comprehend at the time. This is the essential lesson for all who are called of God.

As previously stated, there is a connection between fear and love. Now we see that there is also the connection of *faith*. Day by day, the young but mature prophet will need to decide whether the Lord's promises are true:

> *"They will fight against you, but they will not overcome you, for I am with you to deliver you,"* declares the Lord.
> JEREMIAH 1:19 (NASB)

As believers, this is the challenge set before each of us in this twenty-first century: It's a matter of faith, love and fear. And although we haven't received Jeremiah's calling, the summons to faith may, sooner or later, take us through our own house of *phobos* fear rather than around it. But the Lord's promises have been steadfast throughout the ages. He will prepare us and never leave us if we trust in Him.

FEAR OF DEATH

It's been said that *glossophobia*—the fear of public speaking—is man's greatest fear. But if glossophobia is truly the greatest of all our fears, we would expect Hollywood to pick up on it by now through the entertainment industry. Just imagine a new suspense genre with a storyline depicting an average citizen walking down a public street, suddenly kidnapped by thugs, then forced into a life of public speaking. While many of us can envision the angst of standing before an audience and giving a presentation, such a movie would hardly keep us on the edge of our seats. But maybe glossophobia could be added to the list of Jeremiah's burdens since he had to address hostile audiences on a regular basis.

> ...All those who hate [God] love death.
> – Proverbs 8:36 (NKJV)

Today, we live in an age that regularly celebrates death and violence in various art forms. Hollywood's brand of entertainment never passes up an opportunity to leverage the human emotions connected to our own mortality. Often, the industry's ability to maximize a sense of dread, panic, and fright defines its success at the box office, and each movie thriller in succession attempts to outdo its predecessor. With the assurance of surviving each screen experience, viewers are free to use the cliffhanger to exploit their own fears (for the sake of entertainment) within the safe environment of the home or theater—like facing down an angry tiger perched behind four inch steel bars. But how do the scenes of a Hollywood thriller influence the way we view death? And what are their effects on our emotional and spiritual wellbeing? These can be difficult questions to answer because the average person doesn't go through life thinking only about death. In his book, *Staring at the Sun*, author Irvin D. Yalom puts it this way:

> "It's not easy to live every moment wholly aware of death. It's like trying to stare the sun in the face: you can stand only so much of it."[9]

But when the love and fear of God is supplanted by perverse images of dying for the sake of entertainment, our path to understanding life and death is narrowed. Since our demise in this world is certain (studies show that human mortality is currently at 100 percent), it would seem in everyone's best interest to humbly seek the truth of God when approaching the subject of death. But as Hebrews 12:1 points out, sin easily *besets us*, and we have an amazing human capacity to downgrade critical issues on our list of priorities when they're not perceived as immediate threats. Of course, most people can't tell how close they are to death if blessed with good health. Even so, there are people lying on their death beds who have long embraced a view of the afterlife based on the popular notion: *I'm a good person and have lived a good life.*

> [God] who has saved us and called us with a holy calling, not according to our works, but according to His own purpose and grace which was granted us in Christ Jesus from all eternity, but now has been revealed by the appearing of our Savior Christ Jesus, who abolished death and brought life and immortality to light through the gospel.
> – II Timothy 1:9-10 (NASB)

Life brings everyone to the ultimate point of their own end, and people deal with that reality in various ways. It's difficult to contend with something that's both real *and* surreal to us. In this physical life, death remains a dark

---

9   Staring at the Sun: Overcoming the terror of Death, Irvin DI Yalom, Chapter One, The Mortal Wound, p.5, copyright 2009

void and demands faith for any interpretation of it. Even an atheist's concept of death frames his or her own statement of faith. And regardless of its origin, faith—like death itself—is inescapable.

The strength of one's assurance in defining what the post-death world looks like (assuming the individual believes in such a world), has a significant impact on how that person views death in the first place. To put it another way, our degree of faith (however defined) correlates to our level of fear. But in reality, truth isn't necessarily a prerequisite for faith when it comes to surmounting the fear of death. There are nonbelievers who have expressed a positive attitude at the end of life, and this can seem perplexing to a follower of Christ. After all, the joy of Christian hope is largely defined through faith in the promises of eternal life with God. Yet, the fact remains that there are nonbelievers more dedicated in defending a lie than are some believers in proclaiming the truth. The very act of terrorism provides a striking example of those who embrace death without a sign of fear; but in so doing, they have committed themselves to a lie that defines both their works *and* their faith. In the end, man's allegiances, right or wrong, will always follow him to the grave and to the judgment beyond.

> To him who is afraid, everything rustles.
> – SOPHOCLES, *ACRISIUS*

NEEDLESS FEAR

Once fear stakes its claim in the heart and mind it becomes substantive, and the dreaded emotion that follows is rarely dependent on whether the actual threat is real or imagined. So, the validity of our anxieties can only be confirmed when emotions are held to accountability. Without the burden of proof, fear will continue to hold its high ground, unopposed.

Unfortunately, we frequently rely on emotions as our sole guide through both good times *and* bad. It's easy to believe that current favorable conditions will last forever; or conversely, that bad times will never end. But tidings that seem to announce our deepest fears are often embraced too quickly, as though we don't have time to objectively consider any other report.

One of the many examples of panic overreach can be seen from the first Earth Day ceremony which took place in 1970. This annual event continues to be celebrated worldwide, bringing people together with a common passion for the cause of environmental protection. Of course, the idea of a global threat to life due to runaway pollution, climate change, and diminishing natural resources is enough to concern anyone who happens to enjoy life on planet earth. But the proclamations that came out of that 1970 rally were enough to make people want to climb a high cliff and wait for the end to come—or jump.

The following declarations of doom were offered by several noted and respected authorities of the time. Not one prediction came true!

1. "Civilization will end within 15 or 30 years unless immediate action is taken against problems facing mankind." — *Harvard biologist George Wald*
2. "We are in an environmental crisis which threatens the survival of this nation, and of the world as a suitable place of human habitation." — *Washington University biologist Barry Commoner*
3. "Man must stop pollution and conserve his resources, not merely to enhance existence but to save the race from intolerable deterioration and possible extinction." — *New York Times editorial*
4. "Population will inevitably and completely outstrip whatever small increases in food supplies we make. The death rate will increase until at least 100-200 million people per year will be starving to death during the next ten years." — *Stanford University biologist Paul Ehrlich*
5. "Most of the people who are going to die in the greatest cataclysm in the history of man have already been born . . . [By 1975] some experts

feel that food shortages will have escalated the present level of world hunger and starvation into famines of unbelievable proportions. Other experts, more optimistic, think the ultimate food-population collision will not occur until the decade of the 1980s." — *Paul Ehrlich*

6. "It is already too late to avoid mass starvation," — *Denis Hayes, Chief organizer for Earth Day*
7. "Demographers agree almost unanimously on the following grim timetable: by 1975 widespread famines will begin in India; these will spread by 1990 to include all of India, Pakistan, China and the Near East, Africa. By the year 2000, or conceivably sooner, South and Central America will exist under famine conditions... By the year 2000, thirty years from now, the entire world, with the exception of Western Europe, North America, and Australia, will be in famine." — *North Texas State University professor Peter Gunter*
8. "In a decade, urban dwellers will have to wear gas masks to survive air pollution... by 1985 air pollution will have reduced the amount of sunlight reaching earth by one half." — Life *magazine*
9. "At the present rate of nitrogen buildup, it's only a matter of time before light will be filtered out of the atmosphere and none of our land will be usable." — *Ecologist Kenneth Watt*
10. "Air pollution... is certainly going to take hundreds of thousands of lives in the next few years alone." — *Paul Ehrlich*
11. "By the year 2000, if present trends continue, we will be using up crude oil at such a rate... that there won't be any more crude oil. You'll drive up to the pump and say, 'Fill 'er up, buddy,' and he'll say, 'I am very sorry, there isn't any.'" — *Ecologist Kenneth Watt*
12. "[One] theory assumes that the earth's cloud cover will continue to thicken as more dust, fumes, and water vapor are belched into the atmosphere by industrial smokestacks and jet planes. Screened from the sun's heat, the planet will cool, the water vapor will fall and freeze, and a new Ice Age will be born." — Newsweek *magazine*
13. "The world has been chilling sharply for about twenty years. If present trends continue, the world will be about four degrees colder for the

global mean temperature in 1990, but eleven degrees colder in the year 2000. This is about twice what it would take to put us into an ice age."
— *Kenneth Watt*

The hysteria of that first Earth Day assembly lives on, and creates a climate of distrust in the twenty-first century debate on global warming. But the exposure of these doomsday delusions should not imply that good environmental policies are not worthy of consideration or implementation. In fact, those who love God should care for the earth that He has created. But the care of our world should be predicated on truth rather than fear based on false statements.

The centuries-old classic, *The Boy Who Cried Wolf*, tells of a shepherd boy who repeatedly alarmed local villagers of an attacking wolf. After the locals discovered that the boy was a prankster, they ignored his subsequent cries for help. On the day the wolf actually arrived, the boy was left alone to witness the destruction of his flock.

All the characters in this classic fable understood that wolves represented a real threat to the community. That's what caused their reaction each time the shepherd boy cried for help. But when the villagers decided that they'd no longer respond to the boy's deception, it didn't mean they no longer believed in the threat of wolves; it simply meant that they lost trust in the shepherd boy and his alarm.

Perhaps the eco-doomsayers of Earth Day had a more honorable intention than merely pulling a prank on the masses, but it doesn't matter. Just as the villagers understood the real threat of an attacking wolf, everyone knows that there are credible ecological concerns in the world, and every good citizen—certainly every Christian—has a responsibility to care for God's bountiful earth. But when false claims are used as a cause for alarm, unwarranted fears and misguided reactions only serve to undermine an otherwise legitimate need for responsible ecological management.

The story of the first Earth Day rally serves as an example in principle: Simply stated, fear must be confronted and overcome with truth. Otherwise, fear is misrepresented and thereby empowered through the lie that carries it. Fortunately, there are plenty of historical examples in which the recognition of truth perseveres over fear and leads people to victory.

In his first inaugural address, President Franklin Roosevelt exposed the fears of his day and effectively identified the consequences of yielding to its deceptive anxieties. His famous words can serve as a good reminder that we have a responsibility to ourselves, to our neighbors, and to God, to hold our emotions accountable to the truth and act in faith rather than fear.

> *So, first of all, let me assert my firm belief that the only thing we have to fear is fear itself—nameless, unreasoning, unjustified terror which paralyzes needed efforts to convert retreat into advance.*[10]

So, to revisit the earlier question: Is fear a sin? Yes it is, inasmuch as it's allowed to persuade us to disobey God. Remember, the only valid fear for the believer is a boundless reverence for the Lord and His omnipotence. We should, at least, treat all other fears as a sin, holding our emotions accountable and seeking victory over them.

The full armor of God mentioned in Ephesians 6:10-17 includes the sword— our best weapon. The sword represents the power of the Spirit through the word of God, providing an endless arsenal that both exposes and overcomes fear.

---

10 32nd U.S. president, Franklin Delano Roosevelt's First Inaugural Address, March 4, 1933

BRAVE HEART

This brings us to a point where faith and chivalry must be defined on their own terms, and not confused.

> But Peter said to Him, "Even though all may fall away, yet I will not." And Jesus said to him, "Truly I say to you, that this very night, before a rooster crows twice, you yourself will deny Me three times." But Peter kept saying insistently, "Even if I have to die with You, I will not deny You!" And they all were saying the same thing also.
> – Mark 14:29-31 (NASB)

Regardless of one's sincerity or determination, human courage is not sufficient to fulfill God's grand purpose, and chivalry alone cannot pave the way to accomplishing His ultimate goal in our lives. But as we put on the full armor of God, as mentioned in Ephesians 6, and continually seek the depths of truth behind the shield of faith, we will begin to see death in its reality. And we'll gain a better understanding of our role in this amazing eternal life process.

> O death, where is thy sting? O grave, where is thy victory?
> – I Corinthians 15:55 (KJV)

CHAPTER NINE

Politics and Religion

In the popular sense, the word *politics* can be defined as the methods and tactics used to run a government or an organization. But this simple generic description really fails to capture the significance that politics brings to our daily lives. When compared to spiritual matters, politics is generally considered to be a foreign affair—no pun intended. Such a notion may explain why many protestant churches have long taken the position that politics and religion "don't mix", and should never intersect during a Sunday morning service or any other church activity.

But if we take a closer look at government policies and their consequences throughout our culture, it would be fair to say that politics is intrinsically an ongoing process for implementing legislated morality. Examine any leading foreign or domestic issue in the news today and you're likely to find that it's either directly or indirectly anchored to a moral principle.

In order to adequately make the connection between politics and morality, we must first understand the political divide in America's twenty-first century society. This is not to suggest that our expectations in national polity waited until now to part like the Red Sea; America has a history of split positions. But the rapid change of events and global shift in power, seen in this twenty-first century, puts our current political rift into a unique and dangerous class of its own.

Despite America's cultural diversity, we are essentially a people made up of conservative and liberal worldviews—albeit the purists in either camp do not represent a group majority. In part, the conservative holds a view for smaller government, personal responsibility, strong national defense ("peace through strength"), and a fiscal policy that includes lower taxes to promote economic development through a free market system. On the other hand, the modern liberal generally supports a larger, more inclusive government, a foreign policy involving less aggressive use of the military, redistribution of national wealth, strong environmental policies, and flexible social norms that accommodate equal rights.

Somewhere between these political views resides the moderate who stakes a claim for reasonable compromise by extrapolating a mix of values and methods from both sides. For example, the moderate's political blend may oppose legalized abortion, but support homosexual marriage. Today, a popular compromise takes a conservative position on fiscal policies coupled with a more liberal stance on social issues. The moderate, or independent voter, is subject to a love-hate relationship with his political counterparts whenever he refers to either side as *extremist*—depending on the issue at hand.

In earlier times, conservatives and liberals were more aligned on many important topics: America's role in the world, the sovereignty of major institutions, and a robust free market system—just to mention a few. As the twenty-first century gets underway, the two groups are quickly becoming polar opposites. This phenomenon is not only taking place in America, but throughout Western civilization. It's interesting to note that the things separating conservatives and liberals are almost always seen in their solutions to existing problems, and not the problems themselves. Everyone seems to agree on the headache, but not the medicine.

Another interesting observation can be seen in America's evangelical churches where liberals and conservatives regularly sit side by side in the pews. Under the unspoken law of religious and political detachment, it's not uncommon for one church member to completely be unaware of his brother's perspective on major issues of the day. But if both the conservative and the liberal are attending church, with each one holding the belief that his personal worldview is best aligned with that of the Almighty, then who is charged with the responsibility of providing clarity to the matter?

Over the years, both conservatives and liberals have proclaimed a certain righteous standard for a more perfect world. And although one doesn't need to be a person of faith in order to hold a political view, most people *do* proclaim a belief in God and attach their politics to that belief in some form or fashion. The presuppositions that emerge from such a connection have occasionally been expressed through proclamations (directly or indirectly) that "God would vote Democrat," or "God would vote Republican"—especially during an election season.

For those who see a correlation between spiritual faith and earthly politics, it's essential to understand God's view on the size and role of government, along with the moral implications behind its policies. Is it possible to determine which political party God would support? WWJD?[11] Perhaps the answer would surprise all sides.

We don't need to venture very far into the Old Testament to discover whether the Lord favors a large or small government to rule over its citizens. In I Samuel 8, the prophet Samuel is the acting liaison between God and the elders of Israel. The elders have used the occasion of Samuel's old age, along with the ineptitude of his sons, to petition for a ruling king.

---

11   What would Jesus do?

> *But the thing displeased Samuel, when they said, Give us a king to judge us. And Samuel prayed unto the Lord. And the Lord said unto Samuel, Hearken unto the voice of the people in all that they say unto thee: for they have not rejected thee, but they have rejected me, that I should not reign over them.*
>
> I Samuel 8: 6, 7 (KJV)

From the very beginning, the Lord desired neither a large nor a small government; instead, He desired no government at all. In the verses that follow, God tried to persuade Israel to reconsider their petition for a king.

> *He said, "This will be the procedure of the king who will reign over you: he will take your sons and place them for himself in his chariots and among his horsemen and they will run before his chariots. He will appoint for himself commanders of thousands and of fifties, and some to do his plowing and to reap his harvest and to make his weapons of war and equipment for his chariots.*
>
> *He will also take your daughters for perfumers and cooks and bakers. He will take the best of your fields and your vineyards and your olive groves and give them to his servants. He will take a tenth of your seed and of your vineyards and give to his officers and to his servants. He will also take your male servants and your female servants and your best young men and your donkeys and use them for his work. He will take a tenth of your flocks, and you yourselves will become his servants. Then you will cry out in that day because of your king whom you have chosen for yourselves, but the Lord will not answer you in that day."*

Nevertheless, the people refused to listen to the voice of Samuel, and they said, "No, but there shall be a king over us, that we also may be like all the nations, that our king may judge us and go out before us and fight our battles."

I Samuel 8: 11-20 (NASB)

> Which government is best? That which teaches us to govern ourselves.
> — Johann Wolfgang von Goethe, *Proverbs in Prose*

Today, we could wish that the government would *only* take a tenth of our earned assets as stated in verses 15-17. Throughout the ages, God's warnings have proven true many times over. If only the elders had reconsidered their position and elected to obediently live under God's reign, world history would have a better story to tell. But true to form, Israel rejected the Lord's loving overture and they ended up with a king that they could call their own. His name was Saul, son of Kish from the tribe of Benjamin; and Samuel anointed Saul to rule over Israel according to God's divine appointment.

> Power tends to corrupt, and absolute power corrupts absolutely.
> — Lord Acton, letter (1887)

We might think that the earlier lessons learned under Egypt's oppressive rule would have compelled Israel to lean on the Lord as their governing entity. But the mistakes of God's chosen people represent the mistakes of all mankind. If we stop to consider the divine alternative to human government, realized under the administration of God, it soon becomes apparent that humanity has missed a colossal opportunity.

TYPES OF GOVERNMENT

The more common types of government can be classified as follows:

Democracy — Simply stated, a pure democracy is "rule by the people" with the majority deciding policies, procedures, and protocols.

Republic — Since the management of a pure democracy is impossible in larger societies, the people elect representatives to make and enforce laws. In fact, all national "democracies" are republics.

Monarchy — Rule by a king or queen. Today, there are no large monarchies. The United Kingdom is actually a republic because the queen possesses no real political power.

Aristocracy — Rule by the typically wealthy and educated aristocrats. Today, *aristocracy* carries the negative connotation of a society dominated by the rich.

Dictatorship — Rule by a single person, or limited group of people. Often, dictators resist calling their governments *dictatorships*. They generally refer to them as "Democratic Republics". In truth, they are neither democratic nor a republic in nature.

America adopted a Republic form of government and we, as citizens, have pledged our allegiance to it:

> *I pledge allegiance to the flag of the United States of America, and to the republic for which it stands, one nation under God, indivisible, with liberty and justice for all.*

Despite its unifying message, *The Pledge of Allegiance* underwent a contentious change from its author's original intent. In August of 1892, a socialist minister named Francis Bellamy (1855-1931) wrote the pledge as part of a school ceremony to mark the 400th anniversary of Columbus' arrival in America. Bellamy hoped that his original pledge would represent the covenant of all nations.

> *I pledge allegiance to my Flag and the Republic for which it stands, one nation, indivisible, with liberty and justice for all.*

In 1923, the words, "to the Flag of the United States of America" were added. Then, in 1954, President Eisenhower encouraged Congress to add "under God"—this to the objection of Bellamy's daughter.[12]

Just as we previously considered whether God would choose a large or small government, we could ask what form of government He would prefer above all others. Again, we might be in for a surprise. Understand that these government types are largely delineated by how they define and enforce their own rules of law. But what is God's rule of law, and how does it compare to those of the nations?

MAN'S LAW VERSUS DIVINE LAW

There's a truth in life: If you have a need or desire, and someone comes along whom you perceive can fulfill that need or desire, that person has power over you. The same holds true on a broader scale, and is profoundly demonstrated through government with its massive resources. As the state strategically positions itself as the ultimate provider and problem solver, its citizens become more willing to empower it by relinquishing control of their own lives. Over time, the expansion of laws begins to shape the power relationship between government and its citizenry, leaving future generations

---

12 Historic Documents, *Pledge of Allegiance: http://www.ushistory.org/documents/pledge.htm*

less independent than their predecessors. This is the fundamental process of ceding freedom and prosperity in a nation that has largely been defined by both.

> And [Jesus] said to him, "You shall love the Lord your God with all your heart, and with all your soul, and with all your mind. This is the great and foremost commandment. The second is like it, You shall love your neighbor as yourself. On these two commandments depend the whole Law and the Prophets."
> – Matthew 22:37-40 (NAS)

Imagine if the nations of the earth, with all their forms of government, adopted those two divine commandments of God (stated above) as the foundation for *all* their laws. In such a world, would it really matter what form of government ruled over any given country? Think about it. If every nation embraced the fullness of God's laws of love, then social order, foreign relations, fiscal policies, environmental management, and everything under the jurisdiction of government could forge a universal cohesion to produce peace and prosperity beyond our imagination. In the end, the only significant difference between governments would be seen through their logistical applications for administering the same moral rule.

> Let the heavens be glad, and let the earth rejoice;
> And let them say among the nations, "The Lord reigns."
> – I Chronicles 16:31 (NASB)

As Christians, we live in the hope of such a world when Christ ultimately establishes His kingdom on earth. In the meantime, we live in a global system corrupted by sin whereby man increasingly turns to government to resolve his issues. Nevertheless, God has devotedly prescribed the means for good governance on earth through an allegiance between Himself, His ordained rulers, and society as a whole. When these principles are followed, the nation is blessed.

> *Let every soul be subject to the governing authorities. For there is no authority except from God, and the authorities that exist are appointed by God. Therefore whoever resists the authority resists the ordinance of God, and those who resist will bring judgment on themselves. For rulers are not a terror to good works, but to evil. Do you want to be unafraid of the authority? Do what is good, and you will have praise from the same. For he is God's minister to you for good. But if you do evil, be afraid; for he does not bear the sword in vain; for he is God's minister, an avenger to execute wrath on him who practices evil. Therefore you must be subject, not only because of wrath but also for conscience' sake. For because of this you also pay taxes, for they are God's ministers attending continually to this very thing. Render therefore to all their due: taxes to whom taxes are due, customs to whom customs, fear to whom fear, honor to whom honor.*
>
> ROMANS 13:1-7 (NKJV)

By analyzing each section of this scripture, we can draw some obvious conclusions regarding the divine hierarchy, relationships, and duties of human government:

vv. 1 and 2 *Let every soul be subject to the governing authorities. For there is no authority except from God, and the authorities that exist are appointed by God. Therefore whoever resists the authority resists the ordinance of God, and those who resist will bring judgment on themselves.*

God begins by establishing His omnipotence and authority. He alone appoints heads of state and empowers them to govern. As a result, unlawful resistance of this authority is seen as an affront to God's ordination of power. Such acts will be judged and prosecuted.

> vv. 3 and 4 *For rulers are not a terror to good works, but to evil. Do you want to be unafraid of the authority? Do what is good, and you will have praise from the same. For he is God's minister to you for good. But if you do evil, be afraid; for he does not bear the sword in vain; for he is God's minister, an avenger to execute wrath on him who practices evil.*

This Scripture addresses both the responsibility of leaders and citizens. Since rulers are directly subject to the Lord's divine authority, they are instructed to allow and encourage the good works of the citizens. This is perfectly compatible with Christ's mandate for each individual to love his neighbor as himself. So, the intent is for government to get out of the way and allow its people to do what God has called them to do, while directing its force towards the prevention of evil.

The net effect results in social empowerment; however, it's the government that has the official mandate to "bear the sword" and execute justice on evil doers.

This again protects society and clears the path for good works.

> vv. 5-7 *Therefore you must be subject, not only because of wrath but also for conscience' sake. For because of this you also pay taxes, for they are God's ministers attending continually to this very thing. Render therefore to all their due: taxes to whom taxes are due, customs to whom customs, fear to whom fear, honor to whom honor.*

God's design for a healthy society includes a dedicated allegiance from the people to obey the laws ("be subject") and fund the state through necessary taxes.

Being a law-abiding citizen must result from more than just a fear of penalty; we're called to obey the law for a greater moral purpose ("conscience sake," v.5). The people are reminded that their rulers are "God's ministers" who will be accountable to His ultimate authority.

Like a marriage, the divine focus of government was never meant to create a structure intent on merely seeking power and control over its people. Rather, it was appointed to establish a blessed synergy that glorifies God and makes the world a better place to live.

> For we wrestle not against flesh and blood, but against principalities, against powers, against the rulers of the darkness of this world, against spiritual wickedness in high places.
> – Ephesians 6:12 (KJV)

As we gain a deeper understanding of the spiritual dynamic in the ruling order, we can see how morality serves as an essential bonding agent between God, the state, and the people. A breach in this relationship is most often the result of moral infractions which, left unattended, corrupt both power in government and the citizens' adherence to laws. Soon, an erosion of trust begins to undermine hope for the future. In time, freedom, peace, and prosperity can no longer survive.

> My people are destroyed for lack of knowledge…
> – Hosea 4:6 (KJV)

THE MORAL VOICE

The United States is undergoing what may be the most significant long-term change in its history. In nearly every area of life, Americans are being faced with conflicts over the direction of their country. At a high level, many of these contentions fall under the various headings of capitalism versus socialism, secularism versus religion, right to privacy versus national security, economic expansion versus environmental concerns, and states sovereignty versus federal control. In matters closer to the individual citizen, government mandates are challenging many traditional positions on gun control, birth control, the definition of marriage, human rights, drug legalization, healthcare, and parental rights—just to mention a few.

Currently, conservative and liberal pundits have aligned themselves against one another across the full spectrum of media. Each side presents its arguments with a call to action for a political resolve. But pundits in both political camps have created an interesting commonality through the belief that their position represents the *standalone* solution to today's problems.

Both are wrong!

Remember, the first part of this chapter stated that politics is little more than legislated morality. As we ponder the impact that moral values have on the governance of a social system, we can conclude that without morality (and all that it encompasses) there is *no* standalone political solution to our nation's problems. But the reestablishment of sound morals must be actualized at the micro (e.g., individual) level before it can be realized at the macro (e.g., social) level. This brings God back into the picture, because morality has no meaningful foundation if the state and its citizens do not live for something greater than themselves.

> Our Constitution was made only for a moral and religious people. It is wholly inadequate to the government of any other.
> – JOHN ADAMS, SECOND U.S. PRESIDENT

This is not to say that it's the responsibility of the church of Jesus Christ to declare one political party over another, but if our nation's problems fundamentally result from a breakdown in morality, it behooves the church to address social issues and educate believers on public and political matters from a Biblical perspective as directed by the Holy Spirit of God. Church pastors and leaders who turn away from this responsibility must ask themselves: Who then, will represent the moral voice in the community? Should the government make its own declaration of morality? Or should the popular culture use public media to define what is right and what is wrong?

The fact of the matter is, the church that preaches Jesus Christ has the divine appointment to declare the moral standards of God as they are defined in Scripture. It's not enough to leave this responsibility solely to para-church organizations. Although there are a number of excellent Christian institutions that are diligently working to educate people on the many issues of our day, it remains incumbent on the local church to provide moral clarity regarding current events. This responsibility shouldn't be forsaken for reason of fear or under a false notion that "politics have no place in the church." In reality, politics must be expressed in moral terms according to Scripture, because that is what ultimately defines it. Our interpretation of morality is what we live by each day.

Conservatism and liberalism can only represent ideals, methods, structures and tactics as they relate in the context of a physical world. But both positions are undergirded by a philosophical set of principles that can be addressed in moral terms. If they're not, we will no longer need to debate the roles of church and state. The state will assume the moral voice and use it to affirm its own position of power.

CHAPTER TEN

The End Game

> To every thing there is a season, and a time to every purpose under the heaven.
>
> – Ecclesiastes 3:1 (KJV)

The "war to end all wars"[13] had been won; now, the emerging *Age of Illusion* was seeding a new era, and few people could predict its outcome. The year was 1919 and Jonathan Bell Lovelace[14] decided to give up his earlier pursuits and join his old Army buddy, Edward MacCrone, in a new venture. E.E. MacCrone & Co. was a small but creative stockbrokerage firm in Detroit and Lovelace soon became its "idea man". His dedication, insight and exceptional skills in mathematics helped make his friend's company one of the early pioneers in securities research.

Opportunities seemed endless as the 1920s hosted a major boom in the stock market. These were the days before the general public had any conception

---

13 World War 1 ended on November 11, 1918. The expression, "the war to end all wars" was an idealistic and common belief that became a catchphrase.
14 *CAPITAL: The Story of Long-Term Investment Excellence,* by Charles D. Ellis.

of *economic bubbles*, and investing in stocks was deemed the equivalent to investing in America. This righteous ideal of patriotism helped to supplant any notion of greed.

Edward MacCrone sought to maximize the firm's opportunities by leveraging new debt to the fund's capitalization. But Lovelace didn't like what he saw, and tried to convince MacCrone that the added debt put the firm in a position of increased vulnerability. Lovelace lost that argument and E.E. MacCrone & Co. continued its momentum in building wealth for itself and its clients.

In 1928, Lovelace had become a partner in the firm, and while most executives around the country were in a state of economic euphoria, he saw clouds forming on the horizon. Lovelace's research revealed that investors were buying more overpriced company stocks across the board. Increasingly, the cost per share of many firms, multiplied by their total outstanding shares, exceeded their full business value. In earnest, Lovelace tried to persuade MacCrone to take a more conservative approach in managing the assets of the company, but again, he was unsuccessful.

By the summer of 1929, Lovelace was convinced that the value of stocks was standing on the threshold of a significant decline. He turned bearish on the entire market, began selling his own portfolio, and soon withdrew from the brokerage business. After the infamous *Black Tuesday* stock crash hit on October 29, 1929, the market mercifully recovered somewhat by December. Lovelace then elected to pull the last of his capital out of E.E. MacCrone, and the Dow Jones Industrial went on to lose nearly 90 percent of its peak value over the next three years.

> The situation has been reached in New York hotels where the clerk asks incoming guests, "You wanna room for sleeping or for jumping?" And you have to stand in line to get a window to jump out of.
> – Will Rogers, November 20, 1929

In 1931, Lovelace had resettled in Los Angeles and established his own investment firm, Lovelace, Dennis & Renfrew. His company was the nucleus of what would later become Capital Group Companies; the envy of many investment management corporations in the decades to follow. Those familiar with his success through the market crash called Lovelace "a great market timer". But Lovelace set the record straight by stating that market timing had nothing to do with it. "It was a very simple lesson," he said. "Don't pay more per share for a company's stock than you'd be willing to pay if you were buying the whole company."

The story of Jonathan Lovelace and Edward MacCrone provides us with an example of how people respond differently to changing times and seasons. What causes an individual to recognize coming events while the next person, standing alongside with the same information, seems so unaware?

POINTS OF VIEW

Throughout our lives, we experience many seasons—good and bad, planned and unplanned. During the holiday season, Christians celebrate Christmas because of Jesus' initial entry into the world as a baby *"wrapped in swaddling clothes, lying in a manger."* (Luke 2:12). It's an enchanting yet powerful love story for all humanity, and carries with it the message of *"peace on earth, and goodwill toward men!"* (Luke 2:14). But the imagery of Christ's *second* coming often generates conflicting emotions among believers. Certainly, the idea of Jesus establishing His throne on earth and bringing sanity to this increasingly insane world is foundational to our great hope. However, the season leading up to Christ's miraculous return promises to introduce the most harrowing events in human history. The Bible likens this period to the travail that precedes the birth of new life. And as with the stock market crash of 1929, many people will fail to acknowledge the foreshadowing signs of the times.

Life presents itself as an ever-present taskmaster, placing its demands in varying degrees on the living. In an ironic sense, there's an intrusive nature to the very life we all embrace. At an early age, man seeks to leverage opportunities within each of its seasons in an effort to both survive and prosper. We experience personal sacrifices, endure emotional events, make assessments, form opinions and take action. Through it all, we're compelled to define a personal meaning and purpose in the life we live, and our resulting endeavors will be either within or outside the will of God. In reality, it's untenable for us to function in this world without holding a personal view on whether our physical life portends an eternal life through a higher power.

Once our opinion on this matter is established, we generally exact a position on life's origin and its possible conclusion. Personal interpretations made at this point, serve as building blocks to our core beliefs. And how these beliefs come together—whether through in-depth study, critical thinking, heartfelt emotions, spiritual epiphany or a combination of experiences—is very important. Ultimately, our opinions serve to shape our worldview, which is implemented during each process of setting goals and governing actions. Most often, the way we interpret how life began (i.e. its origin) will have a significant influence in our projection of its future.

On one hand, the Christian belief that God has created the heavens, the earth, and all living things, remains at odds with the secular evolutionist. Not only do the two disagree about the origin of life on earth, they differ on its conclusion. On the other hand, both sides tend to agree that life did indeed have a beginning, and they're in general agreement that the things of this world, as we know it, will end. Of course, many people readily admit that the topic of a global doomsday leaves them flummoxed; but for those of us who *do* hold an opinion on this subject, the vision of an apocalyptic transition to a new life sequel is subjectively embedded in our minds (by faith or by theory) according to our individual worldview. This is where we all bring a philosophy to our opinions.

The secularist view of a global grand finale can vary in a number of ways. Some believe that a cosmic assault in the form of an asteroid, black hole, or super solar flare might cause our demise. Others are more certain that global warming, nuclear war, or a biotech disaster will be the big show stopper. The latter set of options points to the activities of modern man, but as man lives, the debate will continue as to whether these assertions are true. Time will tell. For those who rely on knowledge sources outside of biblical scripture, these doomsday forecasts represent only a few of the perceived possibilities.

THE BIBLICAL RECORD

History authenticates the truth of mankind's insatiable lust for power. With his remarkable capacity for destruction (especially now), it requires no stretch of the imagination to see that he could play a major role in the performance of total annihilation. In fact, the Bible puts man at the very center of what is known as the *Great Tribulation*. This is where sin—that perpetual force—culminates on a global scale and brings humanity to the brink of its very end. But throughout the Old and New Testaments, prophesies also reveal the preseason—or antecedent—to the Tribulation and the return of Christ. At least, in part.

> And you will hear of wars and rumors of wars. See that you are not troubled; for all these things must come to pass, but the end is not yet.
> – Matthew 24:6 (NKJV)

In an effort to gain a deeper understanding of the *end times* (as they're commonly called), Christians often rely on pastors, teachers, and various forms of Christian media to explain the complexities contained within the biblical prophesies. This is especially true regarding the book of Revelation.

Unfortunately, many believers tend to shy away from this important subject because it's too easy to get lost in the symbology of such things as the seals, the horsemen, the beast, the seven golden candlesticks, and other imagery. But the gospels provide us with straight talk and great insight concerning what life will be like during the period leading up to Christ's return to earth.

This chapter will not attempt to interpret the symbolic imagery and sometimes elusive allegories of the prophets; rather, it will largely focus on the words of Christ and the apostle Paul as they relate to the season preceding the second coming. In addition, we'll take a high-level look at major social, economic, and technological trends that have brought us to this amazing point in time. By understanding these trends, we can see how current events unfold to provide insight into the troubling forecasts of Scripture, while revealing the truth of a greater hope to come.

THE TRIBULATION LANDSCAPE

Whoever came up with the saying *you can't see the forest for the trees* successfully captured what may be the all-time greatest challenge to human perception. The message in this phrase expresses the need to step back (from the trees) and see the greater picture (the forest). This time-honored truth also touches on God's message to Isaiah when He informs the prophet that *His* thoughts and ways are higher than those of mankind (Isaiah 55:8, 9). In His omniscience, God sees the trees *and* the forest with perfect clarity and acts accordingly.

But as the chapter on *The Perpetual Force* points out, sin has distorted man's worldview, so he tends to gain a sense of normalcy from only the evidence that appears before his eyes. This trait begins at birth. Whether a child is born into wealth or poverty, a loving or hostile environment, the experienced reality will shape his or her perceptual norm. And unless that perception (good or bad) is confronted by a significant life-changing event, the foundation of that original norm will likely remain intact.

Generally, we modify our perceptions as we mature. But we're never fully prepared to comprehend the greater issues of life and God's plan for the future without *His* revelation. After all, the *trees* that are before us have only been viewed in a state of sin, and that brings us back to the dilemma of failing to see the *forest*.

> ... [God] gives wisdom to the wise and knowledge to those who have understanding. He reveals deep and secret things; He knows what is in the darkness, and light dwells with Him.
> – Daniel 2: 21-22 (NKJV)

God's message to mankind, through the Holy Scriptures, provides us with a view of the forest. It's a broad view indeed, because it covers the full span of humanity and touches on infinity. God's word also directs us to the events of this world (as seen in Matthew 24 and other Scripture) which continually testify to His truths. So, in order for Christians to gain a deeper understanding and a sense of where we are on God's seasonal timeline, we must be attuned to the relevant trends of our day.

TOFFLER'S THIRD WAVE

In 1970, futurist Alvin Toffler wrote the international bestseller, *Future Shock*. In it, he introduced the future to the world in terms that people could understand. In short, *Future Shock* referred to the velocity of social change, brought about by new technologies, which would increasingly occur in shorter periods of time. And his concept of *shock* spoke to the human capacity to adjust to such change.

Ten years later, Mr. Toffler introduced his next bestseller: *The Third Wave*. In the mid-1980s, I came across this book and began reading it. I was captivated with the author's ability to weave the history of manual labor into the present and future, with technology and information as the new instruments of wealth creation. I knew the book's words were applicable to my life and I grew increasingly enthusiastic about the possibilities unfolding before me—so much so that I went back to school while working full time, and pursued a higher education at university. I wanted to be a part of the information processes shaping my company's future. My efforts finally led to an MA in education, with an emphasis in educational multimedia. In time, I was able to change careers and develop training and communication products for my firm. Apparently, I wasn't the only one impacted by Toffler's writings: a fellow named Michael Dell was also inspired by the book and started a company called Dell Computers. Needless to say, his success story is a bit more compelling than mine.

Although the expression *third wave* has been used to describe different things, the author uses it to reference the three major power and economic time periods, or *waves*, from ancient history to the foreseeable future. The book is a study of how increased knowledge and the resulting development of new technologies have impacted mankind. As you might imagine, the social consequences from each wave era exponentially increase in intensity and velocity.

The first wave refers to early man[15] during the agricultural, or agrarian, age. During that period, man's primary resource was the earth on which he lived. The land provided him and his family with space to dwell in; its soil grew food, supported livestock, possessed water, and provided wildlife for human consumption and clothing. There was little need for a marketplace. Family members worked together and their wealth was largely defined by

---

15 Toffler begins with the hunter-gatherer in his first wave time period, but this book will not seek to precede Genesis 2 with the creation of Adam.

their acquired life resources from the land. The family was both the producer *and* consumer of these resources.

Toffler points out that isolated forerunners to technology existed in the first wave world, but there were no means to bring these ancient advancements into a cohesive system. Men sailed the seas, and there existed a few giant irrigation systems; there was even a type of steam engine in ancient Alexandria, but these were considered exceptions of their day—oddities, not ready for primetime.

As the second wave emerged, its impact on the world was tremendous, and sometimes horrendous. This period of time came to be known as the *industrial age* and introduced as the *industrial revolution*. In addressing its cause, Toffler writes:

> *Any search for The cause of the industrial revolution is doomed. For there was no single or dominate cause....There is no 'independent variable' upon which all other variables depend. There are only interrelated variables, boundless in complexity.* (The Third Wave, Chapter 10: CODA: The Flash Flood)

With that in mind, we can look at the invention of the steam engine and its improvements through the work of Scottish engineer, James Watt. Originally designed to pump water out of mine shafts, the steam engine went on to drive locomotives, farm tractors, electrical generators, and it revolutionized the manufacturing process. But, as Toffler notes, the steam engine was only a part (though a large part) of the second wave phenomenon.

The takeaway from the second wave's significant impact on civilization is seen in its "invisible wedge" which it drove between the production and consumption processes of the first wave. According to Toffler, as that wedge created a wider split between the two entities, different people began to occupy the production side, from those of the consumption side. Now, the production group would work to provide for the consumer group through trade. As a mutually beneficial exchange relationship emerged, a dynamic market was born. In time, the invisible wedge "produced the entire modern money system with its central banking institutions, its stock exchanges, its world trade, its bureaucratic planners, its quantitative and calculating spirit, its contractual ethic, its materialist bias, its narrow measurement of success, its rigid reward systems, and its powerful accounting apparatus..."

During my younger days, I couldn't help but notice that a number of folks living in the South somehow remained connected to the events of the Civil War, even though so many years had passed since Lee surrendered to Grant at the Appomattox Courthouse. Occasionally, I'd hear someone opine that the Confederacy would have won that war if they had not been overwhelmed by the resources and armament of the northern armies. Their comments seem to coincide with Toffler's position that the Civil War was not *exclusively* a clash about secession from the Union, or the moral issue of slavery.[16] A larger question hovered over this historic conflict: "... would the rich new continent be ruled by farmers or industrializers, by the forces of the First Wave or the Second? Would the future American society be basically agricultural or industrial?"

Although I agree with Toffler's assessment in practical terms, it would be a mistake to assume that the Civil War was primarily a wave war. The moral position of slavery and the consequences of seceding from the Union cannot be overstated. The course of a young nation seeking to define itself as independent with a formal declaration "that all men are created equal," would be directed by its position on slavery's moral question. America simply could not move forward until that issue was resolved. Nevertheless, the Civil War was indeed a defining moment for the second wave and the future of industry.

---

16 It is important to note that slavery, as far as the South was concerned, was largely a freedom (i.e., the individual's right to own a slave) and economic issue because many farmers relied heavily on slavery as a means of mass production with a low labor cost.

By the time Toffler's book, *The Third Wave*, hit the store shelves, the rumblings of its forecast were already being felt, though not fully understood. The accelerated breakthroughs of new technologies and sciences were beginning to have a social impact as early as the 1950s, after the invention of the transistor in 1947. This remarkable creation set the stage for electronic miniaturization, but the new era of technology was just beginning. In the decades to follow, studies such as quantum electronics, information theory, molecular biology, oceanics, nucleonics, and computational intelligence began to expand man's horizon of space and time while they simultaneously opened access into the smaller worlds of *micro* and *nano* scales.

In 1971, the seeds previously sown for the digital revolution were ready for their first harvest at the public level. IBM introduced its PC 5150 business computer and things would never be the same. By June of 1979, about 100 companies were building home computers. Toffler quoted a retailer in Dallas, "'Some day soon, . . . every home will have a computer. It will be as standard as a toilet.'" Well, in this second decade of the twenty-first century, a home will likely have *more* computers than toilets. And coupled with the Internet, the home computer now puts the world at our fingertips. A boy in Los Angeles may be conversing with his online friend in Belgium while not knowing the name of his neighbor next door.

The digital revolution has really become the backbone of the third wave. Not only have computers redefined our daily activities, the advent of the digital application of cell phones,[17] cameras, audio players, controllers, printers, monitors, and books have created a new reality in how society sends and receives information. Increasingly, anything that *can* be digitized *will* be digitized—including money.

On the face of it, there should be no concern over the replacement of older analog technology with that of digital. Third wave systems continually offer

---

17 Cell phones commonly incorporate the functions of multiple devices such as a camera, audio player, and word processor.

new ways for us to multi-task and work at higher levels of efficiency. In fact, new technologies are generally introduced under the presumption of creating new markets and making life better for everyone. But as we continue to explore the growing contrasts between our past, present, and future, the ultimate questions in life once again appear and beckon us to a deeper contemplation. We're all aware that things are different now, and life is changing at an alarming rate. But it's not the technology itself that's the problem; it's the way that we use it and allow it to shape not just our methodologies, but our views, principles, and our definition of *normal*.

Toffler believed that the "rampant industrialism" of the second wave brought about "a way of life and a way of thinking" which "produced a second wave mentality." This mentality, he contends, was a key obstacle to "a workable third wave civilization." So, the question is: What does a third wave civilization look like? The answer has been rapidly unfolding in our present time.

A lot has changed since *The Third Wave* was an international bestseller. At the time, the Soviet Union was still intact and Toffler believed that the breaking apart, or "demassification," of the predominant media would serve to empower individual citizens. In many respects, he was right. But the politics behind governments has always been about power, and at the crux of that power resides the increasing control of wealth and information.

At this point, there really is no need to address all the changes and advancements that are taking place during the opening decades of this twenty-first century. We already know that technology has brought much more than just digital cameras and cell phones to our lives. Everything from smart meters to global positioning systems (GPS) to DNA sequencing technology is sweeping civilization into a world of unknowns. Information and knowledge birth new technologies; then like magnetism and electricity, reproduce one another. Power is the inevitable result.

THE FORK IN THE ROAD

Through his extensive research and interviews with scientists, manufacturers, military commanders, business and world leaders, Mr. Toffler's series[18] of visionary writings has provided readers with a wealth of information and an extended overview of the rapidly gathering forces that continue to define our new knowledge-driven world. But his conclusions on how the present generation should proceed in this third wave era bring the Christian to a fork in the road. Here, Toffler reveals the direction of his ideological path. He contends that each wave model demands new universal archetypes. It's the call to a new world order, defined by a new world knowledge that is morphing from its past. This becomes apparent near the book's end with Toffler's imaginary letter to the "Founding Parents" of America. In it, he addresses the contributors from our forefathers' eighteenth-century generation.

"You are the revolutionists dead," he begins. The words that follow sing the praises to the collective work of these departed forerunners of liberty. Toffler acknowledges that the "astonishing document" of the *Constitution of the United States* along with the *Bill of Rights* accounted for one of the "stunning achievements" in human history. But though he effectively reveals the significant events and trends of the physical world over the long course of time, Toffler sees little present value in those *stunning achievements* of our forefathers and their application of Biblical principles.

> *For the system of government you fashioned, including the very principles on which you based it, is increasingly obsolete, and hence increasingly, if inadvertently, oppressive and dangerous to our welfare. It must be radically changed and a new system of government invented – a democracy for the twenty-first century ... I come with no easy blueprint for tomorrow's constitution. I mistrust those who think they already have the answers*

---

18   Future Shock, copyright 1970; The Third Wave, 1980; Powershift, 1990; War and Anti-War, 1993.

> when we are still trying to formulate the questions ... we need to join together and reconstitute America.[19]

> Ever learning, and never able to come to the knowledge of the truth.
> – II Timothy 3:7 (KJV)

Amazing! Toffler suddenly juxtaposes the *stunning achievements* of our nation's constitution and Bill of Rights with a thoughtless image of their obsolescence. Then he proclaims that the principles behind these documents of freedom will become *dangerously oppressive* to society's welfare. Such a position can only be accepted through ignorance.

Today, we are the benefactors of the colonists' religious passion which helped build this greatest nation in human history; yet we're becoming more disconnected from the eternal truths behind it all. It's understood that the founders and pioneers of this country weren't perfect, but they largely held to a system of belief in something greater than themselves—a belief in God. That faith became an essential part of the documents of our freedom and system of government.

The great irony in all of this is that the ever-changing world of knowledge and technology is generated by humans whose basic needs never change. After thousands of years, we still laugh, cry, bleed, love, hate, build, destroy, hope, fear, and die. These are just a few of the unchanging characteristics that humanity has lived with since day one. And the idea that the creation of new governments and man-made constitutions can adequately serve the fundamental needs of people, apart from God, is a pernicious lie with dangerous consequences. Society cannot long advance—or even survive—without the foundation of the two divine laws of the Christian faith: loving God, and loving our neighbor as we love ourselves. When allowed, these two factors miraculously serve to define and undergird the spirit of economic theories,

---

19   The Third Wave, Chapter 28: Twenty-First Century Democracy

law and order, power structures, foreign policy, and everything that governs the course of human society.

In order to traverse Christ's alternate (and narrow) path at the fork in the road, we must embrace this understanding. Truth is not redefined by man through his waves of technology and states of knowledge; rather, truth and its workable solutions are built on the reality of God and our obedience to Him. Man only becomes "oppressive and dangerous" when he violates that reality, not because he adheres to it.

But despite all evidence, the Bible warns that many Christians will fail to choose the right path at this critical juncture. Like never before, believers in Christ will begin to face numerous temptations to supplant the truth of God with a newly-declared norm for the twenty-first century, and many will succumb to its pressure.

WAYS AND MEANS

> And [the Antichrist] causes all, the small and the great, and the rich and the poor, and the free men and the slaves, to be given a mark on their right hand or on their forehead, and he provides that no one will be able to buy or to sell, except the one who has the mark…
> – REVELATION 13:16, 17 (NASB)

Years ago, there was a small number of unfortunate Christian B-movies produced to illustrate what life would be like during the reign of "the beast" or "Antichrist" during the Tribulation period. These were strictly low budget films. As I recall, the only thing worse than the acting was the triple-digit 666 branding on each character's forehead. Somehow, I could never bring myself to believe that these well-intended films accurately depicted life leading up to the return of Christ. Besides that, how could an antichrist, or anyone else, accomplish global control over monetary exchanges? After all, it's one thing to make a law stating that no one can "buy or sell" without the "mark," but enforcement of that law is another story. How can anyone, or any government, have the power to stop individual cash transactions, or barter? With few exceptions, the international drug trade continues to demonstrate the futility of such an effort.

But during the brief circulation of the dreaded 666 B-flicks, advanced knowledge hadn't reached a point that would make this ancient prophecy more technologically feasible. Today, digital money is rapidly replacing the use of currency in our daily transactions. In fact, more and more purchases are impossible by cash. Just try to book a flight or rent a car with your fold of dead presidents.

It's not unreasonable to suspect that government will, at some point, implement a move to a cashless means of exchange. In such a world, currency would become totally obsolete. And why not? There are many benefits to consider in a cashless economy:

- Personal convenience—no longer would you need to concern yourself with having enough cash on hand. With the proper digital input, you could effortlessly move through daily transactions, and with preapproved credit, overdrafts would no longer catch you "short on change".

- Personal safety—street crime and armed robberies could be dramatically reduced with the end of cash liquidity. A woman's purse would not be the appealing target to a local thief as it has been in the past.

- War on drugs—suitcases of "laundered" cash, used to move tons of illicit drugs would be worthless. Any digital transactions within the drug trade could (and would) be traced by authorities.

- Global stability—a global digital economy, governed by the ruling body, would no longer need to fear swings in the national currency valuations of sovereign states. This would improve international trade while serving to promote peace and prosperity around the world.

Regardless of whether you believe these assertions, you can expect them to be made (i.e., marketed) in a convincing manner. In fact, these reasons really do provide good arguments supporting an end to physical currencies. But digital money represents a lot more than just convenience, efficiency, safety, and stability in our economy. This "super-symbolic" form of wealth (as Toffler calls it) gives government more absolute control over purchases great and small.

Not only are we witnessing a reduction in the use of currencies across the developed world, we're seeing the rapid growth of information-gathering on a mass scale. For some time, the American people have experienced the collection of their personal data under the common belief that it was primarily for marketing and demographic purposes. We now know better. Recent reports have given cause for concern that the government is extending its reach into the personal lives of its citizens while targeting specific organizations and infringing on their privacy rights. Cover-ups, lies and scandals continue to occupy the news. Meanwhile, the National Security Agency (NSA) has constructed a massive data center in Utah, used to archive online communications and other personal data. The Utah facility—a likely forerunner of things to come—is capable of storing an astonishing five (5) zettabytes[20] of public information.

These illustrations are not intended to demonize government or suggest that one political party is morally superior to another. In reality, politicians from both American parties have supported the idea that government must acquire and use all necessary technology in order to effectively implement its policies. And we have only taken a glimpse at the emerging capabilities

---

20 1 ZB = 1 000 000 000 000 000 000 000 bytes, or 1 billion terabytes

of government in this present age of information. Again, this technology, in itself, doesn't threaten the individual, but the spirit of intent behind it can be dangerous when society and its power structures are no longer governed by a set of ethics, divinely inspired by God. It is this moral deterioration, throughout the world, that the prophets point to as a sign of the end times, leading up to the return of Christ.

POLITICAL CORRECTNESS (PC)

Although the expression *political correctness* (PC) has been used in various ways, it has come to be understood as a common adherence to liberal, or progressive,[21] ideals on today's major social issues (e.g., race, role of government, church and state, gender identity, abortion, marriage, etc.). Furthermore, PC seeks to represent a doctrine of best intentions (albeit with abounding exceptions) designed to elevate minority and disadvantaged groups from all walks of life. In reality, political correctness is an ever-expanding language modifier with an evolutionary trail which is conceived, nurtured, and promoted through influences in academia, media, and government.

Interestingly, those opposed to the term are more likely to use it (in objection, ridicule, or sarcasm) than those who embrace its standard. In other words, politically correct people are much less likely to identify something as being either politically correct *or* incorrect. Perhaps this is because most PC adherents instinctively know the expression is aligned with liberal or "progressive" views which may be diminished if they're associated with a common term that carries with it unfavorable overtones of mass indoctrination. Although PC remains attached to its own stigma, there's an expanding social integration of political correctness into the mainstream thought and language of our day. Its message is continuously delivered and reinforced

---

21   It is political correctness that assigns the word "progressive" to modern liberalism, although Western liberalism itself has been redefined in recent decades.

through various channels of popular media. As a result, political correctness is quickly becoming the new normal with subtle but profound consequences for those who speak or act outside its allusive parameters. One can be accused of being unsympathetic to the rights of women by taking a pro-life position on child birth, a homophobic by opposing homosexual marriage, or a racist by promoting personal responsibility for any and all groups of people.

In a broad sense, PC is something unique in our country. Never before have American citizens witnessed so many attacks against so many things, including religious speech and holidays—especially Christmas. There's even an effort throughout academia to change our traditional concept of calendar time. Annual designators from the historical BC ("before Christ") and AD ("Anno Domini," or "in the year of our Lord") would be replaced with the secular expressions: BCE or CE ("before Common Era" and "Common Era").

The truth is, political correctness is a fool's language, and only a few examples are expressed here. Some incorporate silly and seemingly benign standards for new "appropriate behavior," while others seek to bring down longstanding traditions that have been the foundation of our nation over the years. But all PC examples collectively work to create a new normal and establish common *group-think* for the twenty-first century. And when the doctrine of political correctness has matured and is fully implemented, no longer will any part of it seem silly or benign.

> The Lord said, "Behold, they are one people, and they all have the same language. And this is what they began to do, and now nothing which they purpose to do will be impossible for them. Come, let Us go down and there confuse their language, so that they will not understand one another's speech."
> – Genesis 11:6-7 (NASB)

The Genesis account of the *Tower of Babel* reveals an interesting truth about the power of language when it provides a cohesive understanding among the people who speak it. When that language is confused, the people are scattered (Genesis 11:7-8). In many ways, this social division is also a reality behind political correctness because it confuses language through misrepresentations and multiple meanings. Today, we can see a parallel in the way we communicate (both in America and throughout Europe) to the builders of the ancient tower when the Lord *confused their language* (v.7).

Since Alvin Toffler's earlier writings, the third wave has come to be known as the *Information Age*. It could just as well be called the *Age of Misinformation*. Despite the access we have to daily news, along with real-time data and projections, people have a diminishing level of trust in the information they receive nowadays. The political correctness of our time confuses our language in its attempt to redefine our sense of common understanding, values, and vision. At the same time, critical thinking on major issues is increasingly discouraged. In its never-ending claim to fairly "level the playing field" for all citizens, PC sabotages the individual's capacity to succeed and *love his neighbor* through the benevolence of his own earned prosperity. And like the Babel tower's construction, humanity's freedom and progress will ultimately come to a standstill. This deterioration will be a part of the season during the end time. But the apostle Paul writes to Timothy and delivers a timeless truth; equipping all true believers "for every good work" and preparing the way for Christ's return.

> *But evil men and impostors will proceed from bad to worse, deceiving and being deceived. You, however, continue in the things you have learned and become convinced of, knowing from whom you have learned them, and that from childhood you have known the sacred writings which are able to give you the wisdom that leads to salvation through faith which is in Christ Jesus. All Scripture is inspired by God and profitable for teaching, for reproof, for correction, for training in righteousness;*

so that the man of God may be adequate, equipped for every good work.

II Timothy 3:13-17 (NASB)

JESUS THE PROPHET

Within His ministry as earthly servant and savior to the world, Jesus assumed various roles and communicated a unique message in each one. In portions of the gospels, Jesus takes on the role of prophet and reveals His Father's vision of what the world will be like during the season of the last days. The apostle Paul also provides New Testament insight into this period of time, but we'll begin by focusing on the words of Christ in the first book of the gospels. This is a good place for you to stop and read all 51 verses of Matthew chapter 24 in your Bible, then return to this book.

MATTHEW 24

Christ was with His disciples at the temple, and as people gave their offerings, Jesus noted the heart of the poor widow who sacrificially gave her last two mites (Luke 21:1-5). The beauty of the surrounding area apparently made an impression on the disciples as they were showing Jesus "the buildings of the temple" (Matthew 24:1). But He abruptly rerouted their attention away from the surrounding structures by informing them that there will not be left "one stone upon another" (v.2). Jesus pointed out that, in the grand scheme of things, the temple structures were irrelevant and would be totally destroyed in the end. As you can imagine, this declaration started a big discussion with the disciples, which included a lot of questions.

In the verses that follow, we see that Jesus opened the door to the future, and His words must have seized the imaginations of everyone present—just as they have done with generations since. In verses 4-8, it's interesting to note that Jesus begins His prophecy with a warning to guard against deception in the last days. This is a significant place to begin, because it identifies *deception* as the hallmark of the end time season, and reaffirms the universal truth that Jesus and the Father are one.

For those who don't seek truth, wisdom, and the discernment of current events, the signs of the times will be deemed random, disconnected, and met with a series of misinterpretations. Yet the increase in these perilous and sometimes catastrophic incidents will include wars, uprisings, famines, pestilences and earthquakes around the globe.

But is there really a noticeable increase in frequency of these activities in our present time? As always, people will find a way to debate the issue. For example, there's a recorded increase in the worldwide frequency of earthquakes over recent decades, but one could argue that a greater number of seismograph stations and improved communication networks account for that recorded increase. The same thread of arguments can be made for other end-time events as well. Although the occurrences that Christ foretold are undeniable, man will always find a way to construct an opposing argument based on a common worldview—that is, until reality comes to settle the debate once and for all. But until that time, Jesus warns that these incidents are just "the beginnings of sorrows."

Embedded within the opening verses of Matthew 24, Jesus tells His followers two very important things, and they are seen in verse 6:

1. . . . see that you are not troubled,
2. for all these things must come to pass.

These few words of encouragement seem grossly inadequate when considering the dread that follows: affliction, death, persecution, betrayal, deception, and the "Abomination of Desolation, spoken of by Daniel the prophet" (v.15). If we believe that Christ is the Truth that we seek, then His words must be prayerfully considered and understood.

First, the admonition that we should not be troubled as the world enters its most precarious time in history is consistent with God's earlier instruction for us to fear *only Him* and nothing else. This whole idea is explored in the chapter on *Fear*. It goes without saying, we cannot achieve such a fearless attitude through our own efforts. On its face, the idea of not being troubled during earth's most troubling times is nonsensical without the wisdom and empowerment that comes through God's spirit. The current failure of many Christians to pursue this matter in prayer is a great mistake. Christ is instructing His church to move into this season with boldness, confidence, and strength. He has provided the means to this end and we have the duty to obey.

Second, we may wonder why Jesus said that "these things must come to pass." In previous times, people were always allowed to repent, change their evil ways, and be delivered from impending judgment. Why then, is it deemed necessary for these things to "come to pass" now? What's different?

> And just as it happened in the days of Noah, so it will be also in the days of the Son of Man: they were eating, they were drinking, they were marrying, they were being given in marriage, until the day that Noah entered the ark, and the flood came and destroyed them all. It was the same as happened in the days of Lot: they were eating, they were drinking, they were buying, they were selling, they were planting, they were building; but on the day that Lot went out from Sodom it rained fire and brimstone from heaven and destroyed them all. It will be just the same on the day that the Son of Man is revealed.
> – Luke 17:26-30 (NASB)

In reality, nothing has changed over time. God would indeed heal our land and restore His blessings if people of our generation would humble themselves before Him. But He also understands the perpetual nature of sin, which I have addressed throughout this book. God knows that there will be a time when mankind has fallen into such a state of sin that the only means of restoration is through judgment. History bears witness, whether judgment was confined to a limited region, as it was in Sodom and Gomorrah, or around the world as it occurred during the time of Noah, God's patience has always extended to the last possible option. He is good and His mercy endures forever (1 Chronicles 16:34). In every case, God has delivered those dedicated followers (however few) from His judgments, and He promises to do so again in the days ahead.

WHEN SEEING IS NOT BELIEVING

In the early years of my Christian life, I would often wonder how someone like the Antichrist could take the world by surprise. How could people fail to see him coming? After all, the apostle John warned about "many antichrists" (1 John 2:18) and noted that children of God are led by the Holy Spirit to "know all things" (v.20). For years, the Antichrist has also been presented in the secular world as a character study, through a documentary or in a fictional suspense thriller. With all that's been said about this king of culprits, it only seemed logical to me that everyone—believers *and* nonbelievers—would be more attuned to the signs of the times as they became apparent. Surely, the intensity and frequency of events leading up to the revelation of the true Antichrist would spark a sobering concern in this generation.

But, no.

> And for this reason God will send them strong delusion, that they should believe the lie, that they all may be condemned who did not believe the truth but had pleasure in unrighteousness.
> – II Thessalonians 2:11,12 (NKJV)

The *strong delusion* of the end times that Paul speaks of to the Thessalonians reaffirms the position that there is no standalone political solution to the emerging problems in our nation, and throughout the world. That's not to say that we, as Christians, shouldn't be involved in public life and service of our country. It remains our duty to continually do the good work as honorable American citizens. But we must realize that we're in the midst of a spiritual conflict on a grand scale, and *that* must be our primary focus and passion. All of our hopes to resolve today's problems simply through politics, government initiatives, and other human interventions are in vain. The occasional spans of stability and peace during the end time season will be both superficial and temporary. As world events deteriorate, individual citizens will not be able to deliver themselves from peril through disciplined survival techniques or by stockpiling resources.

Throughout history, in good times and bad, the Lord has called His people to live victoriously through His Truth in this lost world. But that can only happen when we're a people of love—agape love! And it's this mandate that brings the body of Christ to its greatest challenge in the last days:

> *And because lawlessness will abound, the love of many will grow cold.*
> Matthew 24:12 (NKJV)

We know that Jesus is speaking of believers in this passage because of the applied Greek expression: *agape*, the divine and highest form of love, given by the Spirit of God. This verse should strike the fear of God into every believer, because it's *that* love which overcomes the fear of the world. We're not called to cower, compromise, or change our priorities because of current events; rather, we are called to seize the day through the power of God's love. This must be our first priority and pursuit in prayer.

> We have come to know and have believed the love which God has for us. God is love, and the one who abides in love abides in God, and God abides in him. By this, love is perfected with us, so that we may have confidence in the day of judgment; because as He is, so also are we in this world. There is no fear in love; but perfect love casts out fear, because fear involves punishment, and the one who fears is not perfected in love. We love Him, because He first loved us.
> – I John 4:16-19 (NASB)

God's greater plan is at work here, and there's nothing happening on earth, natural *or* manmade, that's outside His control. But if we look to any part of this world system for lasting solutions to the problems it has created, our hope will be lost.

Solomon states it well:

> *The hope of the righteous will be gladness,*
> *But the expectation of the wicked will perish.*
> Proverbs 10:28 (NKJV)

Already, we can see increasing signs that validate this scripture. Across America, uncertainty about tomorrow presents the visible evidence of anxiety that more and more people are experiencing. These folks are our neighbors, friends, coworkers, and family; they need a valid hope that can only come from God. For this reason, we as committed followers of Christ must be in prayer and actively living out the high calling that has been placed upon us through the conquering power of faith, hope, and love. Christian fellowship helps reinforce these virtues.

In its fullest reality, *The End Game* really doesn't speak to the end at all, but to a new worldwide beginning. We must not become discouraged when our efforts don't seem to bring heaven to earth in a big way. Christians alone cannot convert the world's system into the kingdom of God. Jesus will accomplish that grand task when He appears as the victorious Christ. The volatile and unpredictable "new norms" of this world will be torn down like the temple structures of old; replaced with the *real* and *eternal* norm, instituted by the omnipotent God who restores peace, joy and justice for His people.

In the meantime, Christ followers must remain diligent and focused, bearing fruit in every good work. Jesus has laid down the directive: *Do not be troubled. These things must come to pass.*

CHAPTER ELEVEN

Concluding Thoughts

1. Mankind has never been equipped to resolve the mysteries of life, death and afterlife through human intelligence alone. Truth is a paradox which contains both physical and spiritual realities. When we approach God with intellectual honesty and a sincere heart, He makes these things known to us throughout our lives. The apostle Paul touches on this subject in his letter to the Corinthian church:

   > But a natural man does not accept the things of the Spirit of God, for they are foolishness to him; and he cannot understand them, because they are spiritually [discerned].
   > I Corinthians 2:14 (NASB)

2. Our propensity to live a life of faith through the framework of our own assumptions creates our greatest vulnerability. God calls His people to a worldview that's understood through *His* paradigm.

3. Sin has never been a stagnant entity. It moves like a perpetual force that grows with intensity, destroying everything in its path. Just prior to Christ's return, sin will engulf the earth in its full strength. Christians,

should not only *avoid* sin, but hold it in genuine contempt because it represents everything that seeks to destroy an eternal relationship between God and man.

> *Hate evil, you who love the Lord..* Psalm 97:10 (NASB)

4. Although there's a natural tendency to envision a future solely based on the physical evidence of the day, God orchestrates all events. His Spirit beckons us forward with the reassurance of better things to come. In fact, the apostle Paul makes the radical claim that whatever we suffer in this physical life isn't even "worthy to be compared with the glory" that is in our future.

   Can that really be true? The Holy Spirit of God confirms that truth within our spirits if we are followers of Christ.

   > *For in hope we have been saved, but hope that is seen is not hope; for who hopes for what he already sees? But if we hope for what we do not see, with perseverance we wait eagerly for it.*
   > Romans 8:24-25 (NASB)

5. Not only is man incapable of coming to the knowledge of universal truth through his own understanding, he's unable to "abide by all things written in the book of [God's] law." Autonomy is a closed road to righteousness. Therefore, if we refuse the free gift of eternal life provided by the sacrifice of Jesus Christ on the cross, we have no excuse for the salvation of our souls because God has provided abundant evidence on earth and given all of us access to the knowledge of truth.

   > "...Cursed is everyone who does not abide by all things written in the book of the law, to perform them. Now that no one is justified by the Law before God is evident; for the righteous man shall live by faith."
   > – Galatians 3:10-11 (NASB)

Made in the USA
San Bernardino, CA
25 September 2015